CONTENTS

THE DIRTY LITTLE SECRETS

Getting Into a Top College

An Insider's Guide to Admission Into the Top 100 Universities & Colleges in America

PRIA CHATTERJEE

HarperCollins *Publishers* India

First published in India in 2018 by
HarperCollins *Publishers*

Building 10, Tower A, 4th Floor, DLF Cyber City, Phase II,
Gurugram Haryana – 122002, India
www.harpercollins.co.in

First published in the USA in 2015 by Regan Arts LLC.

2 4 6 8 10 9 7 5 3 1

P-ISBN: 978-93-5277-921-5
E-ISBN: 978-93-5277-922-2

Interor design and illustrations by Daniel Lagin

Printed and bound at
MicroPrints India, New Delhi

CONTENTS

Getting Into a Top College

INTRODUCTION

Your GPA is inching toward 4.0. You're on the honor roll. You are a top-ranked athlete. All impressive achievements, but are they enough to get you into the school of your dreams? And what if you *haven't* aced the SAT? Can you still gain a place at a top school?

In *The Dirty Little Secrets of Getting Into a Top College,* I'll give you my unique, behind-the-scenes look at the college admissions process—and the mind of a college admissions officer—showing you what elite schools look for in a potential student. I'll also show you how you can approach this process to minimize stress and maximize success! Through a series of real-world case studies and with the insider knowledge I have accrued through my years as a Harvard alumnus who interviews potential Harvard students on behalf of the university, and as an educational consultant, I'll explain how you too can attend the college of your dreams.

Like life, the college admissions process isn't a level playing field, and unfortunately opportunity and access aren't fairly distributed across society. While there are important factors colleges consider that are beyond an applicant's control, as you will soon see there are many aspects of the process that you *can* control. Focus on what you can control. Accept—or ignore—what you cannot. The college admissions process itself relies on both objective and subjective information. And while it's not a perfect, predictable process, the dirty little secret is that *you* can control several aspects of this process. If you follow a well-thought-out plan and understand the factors, you can construct a profile that will ensure your application lands on the top of the pile.

I'll show you the favored categories of elite colleges, roughly how much of the class belongs to each category, how to best fit *into* a category, and how to maximize your "competitive fit." But it's also important that your college is the right fit for *you,* and we will determine if your dreams are in sync with reality. To illustrate balancing the factors you cannot change with those you can, I will present real-life case studies of students I have worked with in the past, showing you how best to present yourself to the school of your dreams. We'll then assemble these pieces, assimilate these lessons, and craft the perfect college application.

While competitive pressures, costs, and numbers of applicants have risen dramatically, the evaluation process has remained largely unchanged. Admissions officers continue to screen applicants by relying on a basket of factors, including student data (grades, course load, test scores), application inputs (essays, references, interviews), extracurricular activities, and personal qualities. While different colleges might weigh these factors differently, the basic process is fairly uniform across colleges. *The Dirty Little*

Secrets will guide you through this process, helping you present an application that reflects your "best self."

I can make a number of suggestions and explain how the process works, but I cannot implement these steps for you. *You* are the most important factor in making it successful. This is something I will refer to as a "holistic approach" to getting into a top college: Prepare yourself for life (think "holistically"), reach for your "best self" (remember this mantra), and the application process will work as part of leading a positive life. And as in life, it's important that you be *in control* rather than be *controlled by* this often-stressful procedure.

I'll take you through the system—flaws and all—lay open some of its inner workings, and help you design a program that will maximize your chances of being admitted, whether you've been nurtured by focused (maybe even obsessive) parents or are a self-starter, regardless of where you live, how wealthy your parents are, or whether or not you can throw, catch, or run!

Inside everyone is the profile of a college student waiting to be discovered and perfected. All it takes is introspection, objective self-analysis, hard work, finding your best fit, and understanding the system.

If your parents are buying this book before you are born, they might need to be reminded of the importance of the holistic approach. If you are buying this book when you are in ninth grade, bravo. If you're in your senior year, don't fret. *The Dirty Little Secrets* can help at *any* phase in the application process.

So let's get you into one of America's top colleges!

SIDEBAR: A NOTE FOR PARENTS

This is *not* a parenting book. However, since I believe in the central importance of parental guidance in college preparedness, here are a few useful tips for parents navigating the thicket of the college application process.

Empower your children to find an interest and grow with it. Stay engaged and attuned to your child's relative strengths. Encourage an activity that plays to this strength, whether it is a sport, instrument, or artistic pursuit. This can also be a simple, powerful route to building self-esteem. When a child is good at something, putting time into improving that skill will make them feel empowered by their accomplishment, resulting in a commensurate uptick in self-confidence. True self-esteem provides a fundamental building block that helps insulate your child from the stresses and pressures of everyday life.

The outside world never lies: Is your child truly as talented as you believe? Are teacher reports in sync with your perception of your child's academic talents? Do a periodic reality check on your child's relative competitive position and then realign your own perspective and parenting goals. "Everyone's a winner" does not work in the cutthroat world of competitive college admissions.

Beware of delegating parental responsibilities to educators, friends, relatives, or, worse, to children! While we hold education professionals in high esteem, they are overseeing an entire class and are duty-bound to the institution they serve. It's simply not possible for teachers, friends, or relatives to match parental levels of knowledge, concern, and awareness. Set your parenting priorities and be consistent. Be aware that as your child grows, they should increasingly take charge of their own decisions.

CHAPTER ONE

Building the Freshman Class

Everyone is familiar with the expression *You can't fit a square peg into a round hole.* Remember that old saying, because it illustrates how the admissions process works at America's top colleges. Every year the admissions office at a typical top-tier college prepares about 1,600 holes and looks for 1,600 pegs to fill them. They don't evaluate the pegs in isolation, against some kind of ideal standard. They are looking at the different *holes* they need to fill. In other words, if you can figure out the types of students your target college is looking for—types that might be in short supply—you might be able to turn yourself into the perfect peg.

Despite what everyone has told you, from the nice people at the admissions office to your next-door neighbor, the application process is not entirely about *you*. It's important to keep in mind that your dream school looks at an incoming class *as a whole*. You are a piece in a jigsaw puzzle, one that is being carefully and deliberately assembled by the admissions office, and they already have a pretty good idea of what they want their next freshman class to look like. Your job is to make sure you are one of the necessary pieces.

Of course there is room for individual evaluation and selection within specific categories. But the general categories are already well-formed when you apply. In fact, these categories have been remarkably consistent over the past decade, with only slight variations. Each one of America's top colleges has *an ideal class profile,* and its first priority is to build that class.

This sounds anathema to the traditional approach of *work hard, achieve, present your best self, and hope you get in.* It sounds an awful lot like a world of quotas and typecasting. Well, not exactly. Rest assured there is plenty of room for individuality within the eight main factors that determine the ideal class:

1. Race
2. Geography
3. Legacy
4. Citizenship/nativity
5. Family income level
6. Academics and field of study
7. Athletics
8. Extracurricular activities

Of these eight factors, you can directly control and change the last three. But let's focus first on the five factors you cannot change: race, geography, legacy, citizenship, and socioeconomic background. If you understand how colleges evaluate these five factors you can use them to your advantage.

Once you understand this environment, you'll understand the groups against which you will be evaluated, fit yourself into one of the broad categories—or *baskets*—and be competitive and visible within your basket by using the hooks you *can* control.

There is simply too much consistency in the data to think there isn't a pattern to filling an incoming class at one of America's top colleges. This analysis is based on crunching data for the past ten years at all Ivy League colleges and finding a remarkably consistent percentage of students admitted by race, geography, legacy, citizenship, and socioeconomic background. Data released by the Ivies allows us to see a breakdown by academic field of interest as well.

Before analyzing the incoming class, we should note that, using the most recent data, average class size for the eight Ivy League colleges (Brown, Columbia, Cornell, Dartmouth, Harvard, the University of Pennsylvania, Princeton, and Yale) is 1,749 students. Cornell boosts the average with its much larger class of 3,190, which is why we will use a theoretical model class size of 1,600 students.

Across the Ivy League, the average admit rate (the combined admission rate of early *and* regular applicants) is 8.7 percent. Again, Cornell has a considerably higher rate at 14 percent. The average early admit rate at the Ivies for the class of 2017 was around 21.8 percent, and the average regular admit rate was only 6.5 percent.

So the average early admit rate is *3.3 times higher* than the regular rate and, as I will discuss later, strong applicants should consider applying to their top choices early.

DEFINING OUR TERMS

What is a *fit*? A *fit* is the logical insertion of an applicant into a recognizable basket by competitive colleges. Most students fit into a basket but it is the stronger candidates who have "hooks" to gain a competitive edge.

What is a *hook*? A *hook* determines your competitive advantage within your basket and consists of attributes you can control (like academic, athletic, or other talents) and ones you cannot (like race, geography, legacy, citizenship, or family income level).

The admissions office looks at every candidate as an individual and will always make room for a truly outstanding candidate. But they are still making room for that candidate within a class as a whole. And that totality is made up of certain well-defined baskets. For an individual student, the key is to manage the hooks that are within your control and build a competitive profile to differentiate yourself *within* your basket.

Your basket is defined by five hooks you cannot change and that will have a strong determinative influence on your chances of being admitted.

Hooks You Cannot Change

1. Race
2. Geography
3. Legacy
4. Citizenship/nativity
5. Family income level

GENDER

Be aware that there is also a sixth category: gender. We will largely ignore gender as most top colleges today are well balanced between men and women and I haven't found a distinct advantage to being either male or female in the application process (except when it comes to fields of study—those in which women or men are under-represented, creating gender imbalance—but more on that later).

The typical class is about 53 percent men and 47 percent women, although this varies slightly by institution. This means there will be 848 spots for men and 752 for women in our model class. Interestingly, gender statistics for the Ivy League are slightly different from the national trend, which reflects more female enrollees than males. I don't believe that gender provides a meaningful advantage in the college admissions process. For instance, Columbia reports that its incoming 2017 class will be 49 percent men and 51 percent women, putting it closer to the national average.

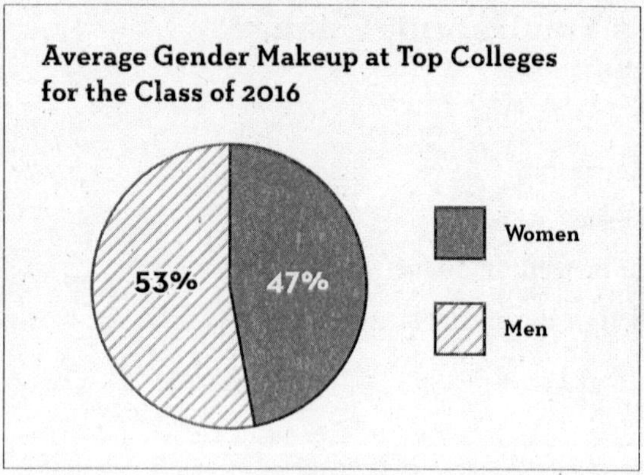

Every applicant can be "typed" into a basket by these five hooks. How does typing work? Let's say you're a bright, young, white student from Greenwich, Connecticut, whose father attended your target college. Add to this profile that you are a US citizen and your family is financially well-off. To the admissions office you look like this:

White—New England—Legacy—US Citizen—Upper Income

That's you, *typed* before an admissions committee knows anything about you. You are now in the *White, New England, Legacy, US Citizen, Upper Income* basket and you will remain in that basket even after the admissions office knows everything about you. That national ballet prize? Your research into T. S. Eliot? You will still be firmly in your basket *and* a ballerina who knows about T. S. Eliot. There is nothing you can do to escape your categorization. So it's important that you navigate to the top of your basket.

Some baskets are at a distinct advantage over others, assuming equivalent academic qualifications. For example, if you are a first-generation Mexican American from rural Wyoming, a resident alien, and from a poor family, the admissions office sees you this way:

Hispanic—Mountain States—Resident Alien—Low Income

It's a great basket to be in. It is a *favored* basket. But a favored basket doesn't mean automatic admission; you still have to fight for visibility within your own basket, despite having the advantage of being in a less crowded field. Like the poetry-loving ballerina, you have no power over those immutable five factors that landed you in your respective basket. But you *do* have direct power over the factors that can enhance your visibility and ensure you're plucked out of your basket and into the freshman class of your dream college.

CHAPTER TWO

Race

Racial Makeup of the Dartmouth Class of 2017

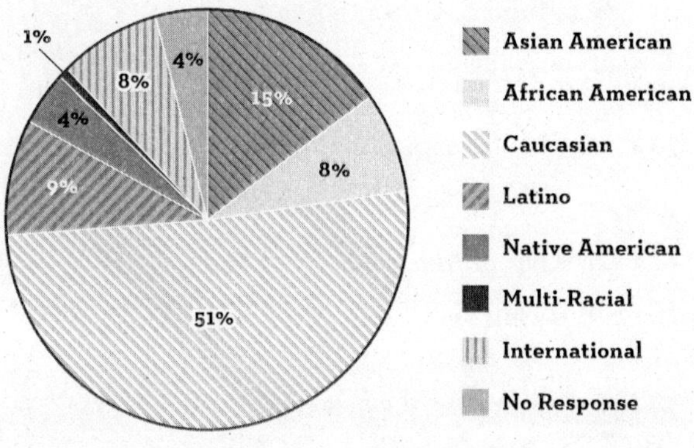

It is worth looking in some detail into how top colleges type someone by race and to see how these determinations can be made to work to your advantage. Top colleges mostly follow the racial categorizations established by the Department of Education's National Center for Education Statistics, which in turn relies on United States Census data. However, there are subtle differences in how top colleges report this information and categorize students, with some using categories not normally recognized by government agencies. These are the categories recognized by the United States government:

1. White
2. Black
3. Hispanic
4. Asian/Pacific Islander
   Asian (reported separately)
   Pacific Islander (reported separately)
5. American Indian/Alaska Native
6. Two or more races

Yale uses the following categories:

1. White
2. Black or African American
3. Hispanic of any race
4. Asian
5. American Indian/Alaskan Native
6. Native Hawaiian/Other Pacific Islander
7. Two or more races
8. Race/ethnicity unknown

Princeton uses a slightly different system of classification:

1. White
2. African American

3. Hispanic/Latino
4. Asian American
5. American Indian
6. Multiracial/Non-Hispanic

Dartmouth is the only remaining Ivy League school to use the slightly archaic term *Caucasian*. It uses the following categories:

1. African American
2. Asian American
3. Caucasian
4. Latino
5. Native American
6. Multiracial
7. No response

Harvard has reduced its system of classification to just five categories:

1. White
2. African American
3. Asian American
4. Hispanic/Latino
5. Native American/Pacific Islander

Columbia uses a similar five-category list:

1. White
2. African American

3. Asian/Asian American
4. Latino
5. Native American

Columbia lumps "real" Asians (presumably Asians from Asia) together with Asian Americans and thus reports a very high overall Asian percentage of 31 percent. In turn, this contributes to Columbia having a significantly lower percentage of white students (39 percent) than Harvard (55 percent) or Dartmouth's "Caucasian" population (48 percent). Columbia also uses the term *Latino* instead of *Hispanic,* while Harvard and Princeton both use the all-inclusive category of "Hispanic/Latino."

Indeed, Hispanic/Latino is the category that seems to most confuse colleges. This is because *Hispanic* is a slightly elastic term and there are a number of people who wish to type themselves as white, black, or mixed *and* Hispanic, such as those from the Dominican Republic, Cuba, members of black minority populations in Central and Latin America, or children of mixed black and Hispanic partnerships. In addition, many people whom colleges, for reporting purposes, type as Hispanic may now prefer to identify themselves as white (like second- or third-generation Cuban, Argentinean, or Chilean Americans).

Given the prevalence of mixed-race Americans, you might be able to present yourself as a "full" member of one of the more favored categories, or you may wish to present yourself in the category "two or more races" (Yale) or "multiracial/non-Hispanic" (Princeton). This latter category is a not-so-subtle invitation to anyone with even distant Hispanic heritage in their multiracial background to identify themselves as Hispanic. Colleges get more credit for being accessible and diverse by demonstrating that they have a meaningful Hispanic population. No one really cares how many students are in the "multiracial/non-Hispanic" category. You won't get a preference for being "multiracial" or of "two or more races."

For purely admissions purposes, it has been my experience that the various "mixed race" categories aren't particularly helpful unless you use them carefully, telling a story that utilizes this aspect of your background. If you are a mixed child and part of your mix is African American or Hispanic, check the relevant African American or Hispanic box. It is up to you whether you wish to also check the "mixed race" box. But be consistent! For example, if you discuss being mixed race in your essay, be sure to also check the "mixed race" box. It's always advisable to coordinate your terminology with that used by the college to which you are applying (although it could be awkward to start your Princeton essay with, "As a multiracial/non-Hispanic student from . . .")

Recent US Census data reveals that many Hispanics, after one or two generations in the United States, now choose "white" for their race. Don't do that on your college application! It can only help to be identified as Hispanic or a member of any other favored minority group. You can see the rather confused attitude to this category in the definitions employed by Yale ("Hispanic of any race"), which seems to suggest that Hispanic is an identity that transcends race. Princeton's category ("multiracial/non-Hispanic") implies that if you are Hispanic you can only be of *one* race. There is, after all, no "multiracial/Hispanic" category.

As with everything having to do with race, there is a significant degree of self-consciousness—even awkwardness—surrounding this issue when it comes to college admissions. My advice: As with all hooks, use your family background to your advantage.

CASE STUDY: Gabrielle from Chicago

Type: African American—Midwest—US Citizen—Upper Income

Background: Gabrielle was a bright African American student at a highly regarded, all-girls private school in Chicago. She regularly placed in the top 30 percent of her class, but never in the top 20 percent. The first time she took the SATs she scored in the mid- to high 600s on each component. Good, but not great. Her class numbered only fifty girls, all of whom were smart and had parents who chose this all-girls high school believing it offered the best possible education and the best chance of fast-tracking their kids into a top college. Gabrielle was one of only two African Americans in her class, alongside twenty Asian Americans and five Hispanics. The remainder was white.

Challenge: While Gabrielle was a strong student, she was nowhere near the strongest student in her high school class. On grades and SAT scores alone, there were fifteen students who easily outshined her. Competitive schools have strong links with college admissions offices and recommend the stronger girls to the top colleges. Gabrielle needed to strengthen her fit by finding the right hook.

Plan of Action: Gabrielle's parents had both attended graduate school and were determined to ensure that their children attended top colleges. Early on Gabrielle's father noticed that she was a fast runner, and by eighth grade she was regularly competing in 200- and 400-meter events. She did well but wasn't a standout star. When Gabrielle's father insisted her coach let her run in different events, she found herself consistently winning in 800-meter events. She had found her distance.

Gabrielle eventually became a nationally ranked 800-meter runner, clocking one of the best times for any high school runner in the country. Despite never academically breaking into the top level at her high school, her athletic excellence, combined with her status as an African American woman attending a top all-girls school, made her a very competitive candidate. Since she did not require financial aid, Gabrielle found herself in a highly desirable basket. The final touch? The emphasis on her academic interest in math. Her parents understood that focusing on a field where African American women were underrepresented provided a distinct admissions advantage.

Solution: Gabrielle presented herself as that rare applicant: an African American female with a strong interest in math and a high level of achievement as a nationally ranked track star. And one who didn't require financial aid.

Result: Gabrielle was admitted to every Ivy she applied to—and to Stanford University.

How Much of a Factor Is Race in the Composition of the Class?

Looking specifically at race categorization in our model Ivy League class of 1,600 students, we find that most top colleges have classes with about 10 percent African American students, or approximately 160 students. If the African American admit rate was even as much as 25 percent higher than it would be without any affirmative-action preference, only 120 slots out of the class of 1,600 would have gone to African Americans. This would mean, mathematically, that 2.5 percent of the entire class (the "extra" 40 African Americans out of our total 1,600 students who presumably benefited from a preference) was admitted "unfairly." But who is to say that the 2.5 percent of "unfairly" admitted African Americans were ranked lower or higher than "unfairly" admitted legacies? Such presumptions also ignore the potential of other factors affecting admissions decisions. Some of those African American students could also have been legacies or exceptional athletes.

At the end of the day, the arguments against a meaningful preference for African American students look thin when measured against the small number who actually end up attending elite institutions. An analysis of racial preferences favoring Native Americans yields an even smaller number that certainly cannot be blamed for tipping the scales against many non–Native American applicants.

Racial preferences affect the absolute margins of a class's makeup, and it is hard to make a strong case that that many students who should have been accepted were unfairly rejected.

THE ASIAN BATTLEFIELD

Top colleges don't like talking about their Asian student admissions policies. Many of these same colleges once had explicit caps on Jewish enrollment (of about 20 percent) and it has become something of a cliché that Asians are the "new Jews"—victims of their own academic success. So it's perhaps no coincidence that there seems to be roughly a 20 percent cap on Asians at many elite colleges.

And that 20 percent may be a kind of tipping point at which a group becomes highly noticeable for competitive colleges. Data shows that, as a group, Asians outperform on both tests and grades. At Berkeley, where admissions are based strictly on grades and scores, Asians comprise about 44 percent of the class. Keep in mind that this does not even include the Asians who are part of the 10 percent international student count. If you're Asian American and a top student, it would seem like a good idea to include Berkeley in your college application list!

But the reality is a little bit more complicated.

Asian Americans make up less than 6 percent of the US population but account for about 20 percent of the class at most top colleges. At Berkeley, part of the University of California system where admissions are based almost purely on academic qualifications, Asian Americans are a full 44 percent of the student population. While many deny that the Ivies and other top colleges artificially limit the number of Asian students at their institutions, the Berkeley example is hard to ignore.

According to the Census Bureau, the American population in 2012 was 13 percent black and 17 percent Hispanic. Both groups are underrepresented at the nation's most competitive colleges. Recent figures from Yale University put the African American student population at only 7.5 percent of the total undergraduate student body, with Hispanics at 11.4 percent. So despite policies favoring these two minority groups, top colleges are nevertheless having trouble finding "enough" African Americans and Hispanics to reflect their share of the general population.

On the other hand, these colleges have had no difficulty finding three times the representative share of Asian Americans.

This is largely due to the fact that the Asian population's academic qualifications have been consistently better than their non-Asian peers. Yale, which publishes detailed information about the racial makeup of its undergraduate population, is a perfect case in point. In 2002–2003, Yale had a total of 712 Asian undergraduates (out of 4,855 students), for a percentage of 14.6 percent. By 2013–2014, this number had risen to 892 (an increase of 25 percent over a decade), with a total Asian student population of 18.4 percent. Meanwhile, the African American student population actually *declined* in the same period of time, from 420 (8.6 percent) to just 364 (7.5 percent), while the Hispanic student population jumped from 6.4 percent to 11.4 percent.

CHAPTER THREE

Geography

Geographical Makeup of the Dartmouth Class of 2017

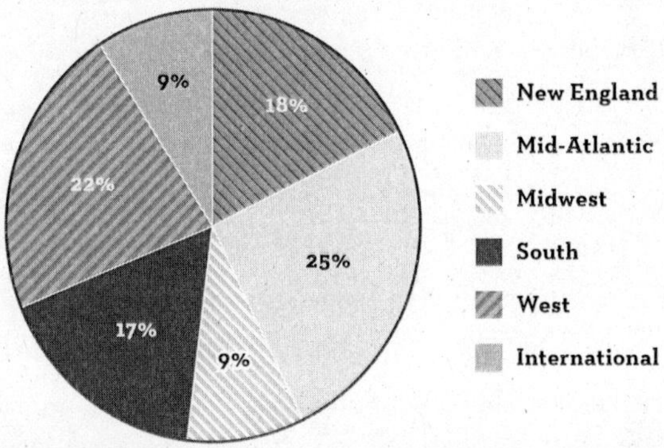

For years, candidates from the Northeast (and New York City in particular) were thought to face tougher odds in the competitive application process. With the steady increase in applicant numbers, Ivy League acceptance rates by state are now more uniform, although differences in the quality of public schools by state do continue to affect the spread. In general, this hook can still work if you are from a low applicant volume area favoring applicants who might benefit from the following demographic data:

THE 10 SMALLEST STATES BY SCHOOL-AGE RESIDENT POPULATION (2012)

State	Resident School-Age Population
1. District of Columbia	71,000
2. Vermont	93,000
3. Wyoming	97,000
4. North Dakota	108,000
5. Alaska	132,000
6. South Dakota	145,000
7. Delaware	149,000
8. Montana	161,000
9. Rhode Island	163,000
10. New Hampshire	212,000

Conversely, you'll have a harder time coming from the largest states by resident school-age population.

THE 10 LARGEST STATES BY SCHOOL-AGE RESIDENT POPULATION (2012)

1. California	6,699,000
2. Texas	5,044,000
3. New York	3,096,000
4. Florida	2,931,000
5. Illinois	2,248,000
6. Pennsylvania	2,202,000

7. Ohio	1,969,000
8. Georgia	1,815,000
9. Michigan	1,691,000
10. New Jersey	1,499,000

To put these numbers into perspective, California has almost seventy times the number of students as Wyoming. This doesn't necessarily mean you are seventy times more likely to get into a top college if you are from Wyoming, all else being equal, but you are probably at least twenty times more likely. With student numbers dramatically smaller from "small states" and pressure on colleges to have a geographically diverse class, well-qualified students from the "smallest ten" are often at a competitive advantage.

Despite this edge, the numbers of students from the smallest ten states are still shockingly low. Princeton, for example, reports the number of students from each state making up its incoming class. Looking at the latest data, we see that four states—Montana, Wyoming, North Dakota, and Iowa—haven't sent *a single student* to Princeton. And the following states also have surprisingly low representation:

1 Student

Kentucky

2 Students

Rhode Island

New Mexico

Wisconsin

New Hampshire

3 Students

Vermont

Delaware

4 Students

Utah

Nebraska

West Virginia

5 Students

Nevada

Kansas

Oklahoma

Mississippi

Indiana

Your chances of actually meeting one of the four students from Utah at Princeton are pretty low, raising interesting questions on the realized benefits from "geographic diversity."

At the other end of the scale, these states send the most students to Princeton:

New Jersey: 204

California: 150

New York: 146

Pennsylvania: 58

Maryland: 54

Approximately 40 percent of the Princeton class comes from just these 5 states. This is not to suggest that you should uproot your family and move to Montana. But it does demonstrate the skewed geographic distribution of students at competitive colleges and how your home state (or country) can affect your chances of acceptance.

CHAPTER FOUR

Legacy

For an Ivy League school, a *legacy* is typically defined as a student who has at least one parent who attended their college as an undergraduate. Some selective colleges (UPenn and Stanford, for example) extend the legacy connection to parents who have attended any of the university's graduate schools. The legacy hook is especially controversial, often viewed as an advantage that says more about an applicant's class and family background than academic suitability.

At selective colleges, there's a potential advantage in being a legacy. But I stress the word *potential* because legacy alone isn't the powerful factor it once was, when underqualified students were granted preference based on the accomplishments of their parents. Indeed, college admissions have simply become too competitive to give all legacies an equally weighted hook.

What remains powerful, though, is the *Connected Legacy*. A legacy becomes a Connected Legacy when parents or a family involve themselves in the college. This involvement might include volunteering an extraordinary amount of time and effort to college outreach and other such activities, and it often does mean financial generosity.

Legacy can be an effective hook when added to an already outstanding candidate, producing a powerful "Combo" or "SuperCombo."

What Is a Combo? What Is a Supercombo?

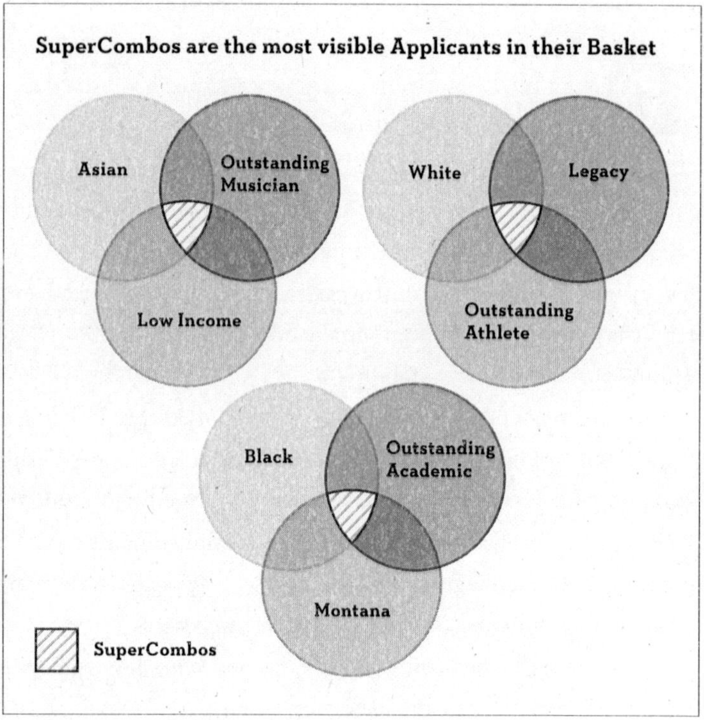

A *Combo* is an applicant with a combination of effective hooks. *SuperCombos* are students who sit at an intersection of three or more hooks, such as the outstanding student and exceptional athlete who also happens to be a legacy. SuperCombos are the rare outstanding applicants able to take full control of the competitive admissions process. They rise to the top of their baskets, enjoying the benefits of much clearer visibility as a result of multiple hooks.

In other words, the SuperCombo is a shoo-in candidate.

Legacy + Outstanding Candidate = SuperCombo

For "Standard Strong" candidates, legacy alone might be enough of an added hook to make for a strong Combo.

What Is a Standard Strong Candidate?

Most competitive college applicants fit into this category: good grades (GPA above 3.7), challenging curriculum, good test scores (SATs above 700), good school-level activities (newspaper, varsity sport, student government), and good recommendations. With these credentials you'll be viewed as a very good student, but absent other factors you'll be indistinguishable from the bulk of talented applicants to competitive colleges.

You're probably a strong fit in your basket but not among the few floating at the very top. You are a very good student but not outstanding. Since many applicants to top colleges would meet these qualifications, this pool comprises about 30,000 talented students every year. Standard Strong alone might not open the gates to the Ivy League but it's nevertheless a solid credential. It's useful to remember that there are about 16,000 Ivy slots, so the odds aren't bad that you'll get into a competitive college as a Standard Strong student. In fact, your odds are about 1 in 2. Furthermore, you have an excellent chance of being accepted to a great—though somewhat less competitive—college. These colleges (often referred to as "safety schools") recognize that a Standard Strong student enhances their overall academic profile.

Legacy + Standard Strong = Possible Strong Combo

For the medium achiever, however, it is the Connected Legacy hook that provides the much-needed push into desirable Combo territory.

Connected Legacy + Medium Achiever = Strong Combo

While it is true that legacy children enjoy a benefit most other applicants don't, particularly at top colleges, the extent of this benefit is by no means evenly distributed. At a top college, with an overall admit rate of 6 percent, legacies might enjoy an admit rate around three times higher: about 18 to 20 percent. While hard data on legacy admit rates is difficult to come by, some colleges make available partial information from which we can infer approximate numbers.

Dartmouth reported that 14.3 percent of the 1,117 students in the class of 2017 are "sons and daughters of Dartmouth alumni." This means that there are 160 legacy students enrolled in the class. Since the overall reported admission rate for Dartmouth for the class of 2017 was 10.4 percent out of 22,428 applicants, 2,332 students were admitted. Of these, only 1,117 actually enrolled, aligning perfectly with the reported yield of 48 percent. This means that only about 5 percent of total applicants ended up enrolling in the class of 2017. If the 160 enrolled legacy students also reflected the 5 percent overall enrollment yield, 3,200 legacies would have to have applied to result in a yield of 160 enrolled legacies. Therefore, it is almost certain that the admit rate for legacies is higher than the overall admit rate. Given that many legacy applicants are from high-income and high-achieving backgrounds, with access to privileged educational and extracurricular inputs, it is inaccurate to say that all of those who qualify as legacies don't deserve their spots. Many legacies are strong students with exceptional grades and impressive test scores. They tend to accumulate extensive and worthy extracurricular activities, both in intellectual and athletic areas. These students are also likely to

Percentage of Legacy vs. Non-Legacy Students for Dartmouth Class of 2017

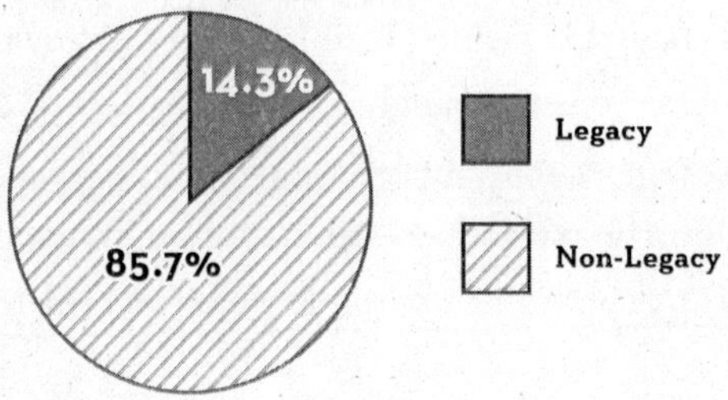

enjoy the benefits of focused parenting, which helps package them as competitive students.

If Dartmouth's legacy admit rate results in legacies comprising about 14 percent of the entire class, the effect of the legacy hook is probably most unfair at the very margins of candidate acceptability, accounting for relatively few egregious cases of favoritism. The actual effect of a legacy benefit is negligible. But for a Standard Strong candidate, it could very well serve as a crucial tiebreaker.

An example of how the Connected Legacy works can be seen in Harvard's use of the "Z-list"—legacy applicants who are guaranteed admission after a required gap year to enhance their college readiness. The Z-list represents the collision of an objective admissions system (or, at least, an admissions system that wants to be *seen* as objective) and the most connected and wealthy alumni.

With the Z-list, the admissions process has found a way to placate a very important constituency (wealthy alumni who are major donors) without appearing to mandate the admission of underqualified students for financial purposes. By attaching terms and conditions before a legacy applicant can gain admission, the Z-list process is essentially acknowledging that the applicant isn't *currently* qualified. Z-listing is a calculated bet that a gap year will be used in a suitable fashion to enhance the legacy student's college readiness. Not surprisingly, almost everyone on the Z-list can afford to do something interesting during this crucial gap year. Who wouldn't be more interesting after building houses for the poor in Rwanda or taking hunting lessons from the Inuits of Hudson Bay?

Using the Dartmouth example, even if the legacy admit rate is substantially higher than the normal admit rate, only a relatively small portion of the 160 legacy admits would not be there if "normal" standards applied to them. The entire debate about the unfairness of legacy admits is not particularly determinative for the entire class, taken as a whole.

Another category that works much like the legacy hook, but with far smaller numbers, is the admissions preference enjoyed by children of college faculty and staff. As with all other hooks and favored categories, the point is to take advantage of this preference if you were fortunate enough to be born of a parent who is a professor or administrator at a top college.

CHAPTER FIVE

Citizenship

We know that citizenship is an important area for colleges and is a category where colleges can give themselves credit for admitting permanent residents (who in some cases are Hispanic children of noncitizens) or other special cases, such as children of political refugees.

Colleges believe that having a distribution of about 10 percent foreign students (and as high as 13 percent at Columbia) is useful from a diversity, reputation, and financial point of view, as many foreign students are well-off and pay "full freight." For example, at state colleges like the University of California, full-fee-paying foreign students enjoy favored access for their financial value because their higher tuition fees subsidize the lower fees charged to state residents. These financial inputs directly benefit the university's bottom line, which is constantly under pressure from state budget cuts. According to journalist Dan Golden, "polo recruits" have enhanced the University of Virginia's geographic diversity and finances by attracting wealthy, "polo-playing" foreign applicants (and potential donors) from countries including Malaysia, Colombia, and the United Kingdom.

Only six colleges (Harvard, Yale, Princeton, Dartmouth, MIT, and Amherst) offer "need-blind" access—in which an institution doesn't take a student's financial situation into consideration—to foreign students requiring financial aid. In rare cases, some colleges earmark scholarships for students from particular geographic areas—like Wesleyan University's Freeman Asian Scholarship, which helps subsidize students from select Asian countries.

Whether for their "snob value" or financial value (well-off foreign students) or athletic value (Canadian ice hockey players or Australian rowers), international applicants can enjoy the citizenship/nativity hook and favored access to competitive colleges.

As with geographic diversity within the US, international diversity is not an equal hook for all foreign students. Traditionally, there has been a slight bias toward students from the Anglosphere (the UK, Canada, Australia), who count as foreign while not having any language or cultural difficulty attending a top US college. And remember, these colleges are concerned with keeping up their graduation rates, which are very—some might say artificially—high. Admitting students with language issues can potentially hurt those statistics, so a student from Canada offers a pretty safe bet to graduate while also counting as foreign in the much-managed 10 percent foreign student allocation.

With the steady increase in applications from high-volume

countries such as South Korea, India, and China, students applying from these countries face tougher odds as international applicants. In general, when international is also considered unusual, the diversity benefit is more powerful. We have demographic data on the foreign student populations at Princeton and UPenn, which have enrolled students from an impressive fifty and seventy countries, respectively. If you are from one of the countries that has not made this list (we noticed Princeton currently has someone from Tanzania but is still looking for someone from Fiji), you could benefit from the citizenship/nativity advantage.

Where Do Foreign Students Come From?

Based on information compiled by the Institute of International Education, the largest percentage of foreign students comes from Asia, with a full 49 percent hailing from just three countries: China, India, and South Korea. Europe accounts for 12 percent, Latin America for 9 percent, the Middle East 6 percent (almost all from Saudi Arabia), Africa 5 percent, and Canada 3 percent. Australia accounts for less than 1 percent of all foreign students.

If 5 percent (of the international student allocation of 10 percent) in our model class is from Africa (and assuming all of those students are black), that would still account for only eight black African students. As you can see, the overall effect of the foreign students is marginal on the black and Hispanic student populations. Foreign students do make up a more meaningful part of the Asian allocation, particularly at colleges like Columbia where they are tallied as part of the Asian American student population. Whether you present yourself as Asian or Asian American typically will make little difference. Either way, as a "foreign" Asian applicant, you are in the most competitive citizenship/nativity category.

CHAPTER SIX

Family Income Level

Socioeconomic diversity (or income-level diversity) generally favors candidates from low-income families. Former Dartmouth admissions officer Michele Hernandez explains that the college's policy favors applicants from the Northeast states of Vermont, New Hampshire, and Maine because "these applicants are rural, less affluent, and white." Top colleges have a difficult time finding enough low-income students capable of completing the four undergraduate years. We can see this in some recent statistics. In 2011, the percentage of high school graduates enrolled in college on a national basis, sorted by income group, were as follows:

Low income	52 percent
Middle income	66 percent
High income	82 percent

There is a gaping 30-percentage-point gap between enrollment among high- and low-income.

Family Income Level—Harvard Class vs. US Population

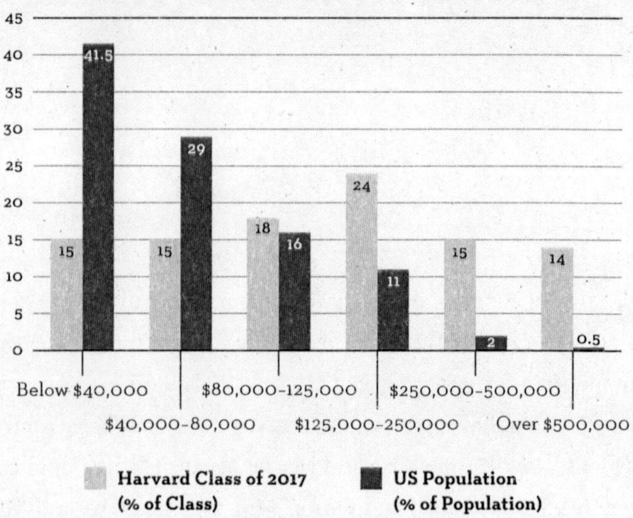

CASE STUDY: Ryan from New London, New Hampshire

Type: White—New England—US Citizen—Low Income

Background: Ryan attended a small, homogenous public high school where he excelled in the sciences. He was a focused, academic student with little exposure to life outside his immediate community. His public school didn't come close to matching the course and extracurricular offerings at nearby prosperous private schools.

Challenge: As a budding computer scientist, Ryan was up against a talent pool filled with "math nerds" and "Asian geniuses." How could he compete for visibility?

Plan of Action: Surprisingly, small, relatively remote American public schools are favored by mainland Chinese families looking to expose their children to a Western education. Smaller, quieter communities are considered safer and culturally less threatening while still providing the all-important English language skills considered necessary for future success. Several New London families played host to Chinese students attending Ryan's high school. Not surprisingly, Ryan and his Chinese friends shared similar academic interests. Sheng came to New London from Guangzhou. Like Ryan, he excelled in math and science. Both boys signed on to the most challenging courses available and shared computing tips and ideas. By tenth grade, the boys had developed an innovative iPhone app and were considering how to transform a hobby into a business.

Ryan had been exploring computer-programming courses at nearby colleges. Although Sheng shared Ryan's interest in advanced learning, he found college offerings confusing and struggled to understand which high school courses satisfied college-course prerequisites. Responding to his friend's need for clarity, Ryan developed a "cyber notice board" to post information on specific courses. Since Ryan and Sheng lived at opposite ends of town, there was also a chat feature allowing for private discussion between them. As word of the program spread, Ryan and Sheng responded by building a more sophisticated app with wider applications, and soon they were connecting peers with various extracurricular opportunities available in the surrounding area. Both boys used their computing skills to build an app that addressed a specific need among their peers.

Solution: Ryan stumbled into a unique pursuit that allowed him to bypass the constraints of his high school's limited offerings. As the popularity of his app spread, classmates benefited from its use and were exposed to outside extracurricular opportunities. And with the growth of the software, Ryan was thrust into a position of responsibility and leadership. His association with Sheng—and other Chinese students in the area—had the benefit of bringing him close to a culture very different from his own. And he accomplished all this without crossing borders or venturing more than a few miles from his New London home.

Ryan was able to "go deep" in his area of strength (computer programming) and enhance his competitive fit as an outstanding talent and young entrepreneur.

Result: Ryan was admitted early to MIT.

FAMILY INCOME LEVEL

Socioeconomic factors can also influence a family's choice of school. While the majority of college-bound students attend public schools (for Harvard's incoming class in 2014, 60 percent of students attended public schools), private schools have traditionally been considered incubators for America's most competitive colleges. As with Asian American achievers, there may now be some reverse discrimination against privately educated students in the competitive college application process. Students are also "typed" by the kind of school they go to. The "private school" basket is more competitive than other baskets that may include "home school," "public school," or "religious school."

CHAPTER SEVEN

The Five Factors You Cannot Change

Now that we have seen what these five categories—race, geography, legacy, citizenship/nativity, and family income level—mean to colleges, we can start to see how a typical class breaks down. Our model class of 1,600 students will break down roughly as follows:

By Race

African American:

10 percent

85 African American men

75 African American women

Hispanic:

11 percent

93 Hispanic men

83 Hispanic women

Asian American:

20 percent

170 Asian men

150 Asian women

Native American:

2 percent

17 Native American men

15 Native American women

Native Hawaiian:

1 percent

9 Hawaiian men

7 Hawaiian women

White:

56 percent

475 White men

421 White women

This gives you an approximate picture of how many of "your" type are being sought for the class. Again, I should reinforce that these numbers have stayed remarkably steady for ten years, so it's highly unlikely that this is a coincidence. Hard data on how much race determines an applicant's success is hard to come by, but admit rates for blacks, Hispanics, Native Americans, and Native Hawaiians are slightly higher than the overall rate for all applicants, while acceptance rates for Asians are lower and for whites about equal to the overall rate.

If we posit that there are 475 slots for white men and you end up the 476th white applicant, you would have to be extraordinarily special to get a spot—and chances are you won't be, because the extraordinarily special white men got spots 1 through 100, very strong ones snagged 101 through 300, and various other special cases grabbed the remaining places. The only way you are getting in as white male No. 476 would be if there were a larger than average number of "supertalented, can't-refuse white men" in your year (and a correspondingly lower number of talented members of *all* the other groups in that year), justifying an exceptional readjustment of the numbers.

In reality, there's an approximately 2 to 5 percent flexibility level in each category. For example, the Asian American enrolled population at Harvard over the past ten years has hovered between 17 and 22 percent—but it doesn't hover between 15 and 25 percent. As with all groups, the Asian range is quite defined. Factoring in a 5 percent variability in the white male category, the number admitted could vary by up to 23 students every year. But this is about the limit on flexibility, as all groups need to be represented via an explicit (or, more likely, a tacit) admissions policy that has changed little in recent years.

This is what *building the class* really means.

By Geography

Based on data from all the Ivies, we have a pretty good sense of where our 1,600 students will come from. They will come from the following areas in roughly the following percentages and numbers:

Mid-Atlantic states: 22 percent (352)
Western and Mountain states: 21 percent (336)
Southern states: 19 percent (304)
New England states: 17 percent (272)
Midwestern states: 10 percent (160)
Foreign/US territories: 11 percent (176)

Now we can apply the filter of geography to the numbers for the categories derived earlier. For our example, let's use the Mid-Atlantic states.

Mid-Atlantic African American men: 19
Mid-Atlantic African American women: 17

Mid-Atlantic Hispanic men: 21
Mid-Atlantic Hispanic women: 18

Mid-Atlantic Asian American men: 37
Mid-Atlantic Asian American women: 33

Mid-Atlantic White men: 104

Mid-Atlantic White women: 93

There will be variations in these numbers, of course. For instance, there will likely be fewer Hispanics from the Midwest than the West or South, but we still get the general picture.

Our model class will have 104 white men from Maryland; Washington, D.C.; Pennsylvania; New Jersey; and New York. This number may seem low, but when you crunch numbers by race, gender, and geography, there simply aren't that many slots for each type of student.

Get Me in Here

This is how a typical top college builds its class. If you are fortunate enough to benefit from any of these five unchangeable hooks, take advantage of them. While you cannot change your race, geography, legacy connection, citizenship, or family income level, you *can* control how they are viewed by admissions officers.

But we need to look at how you can best use *all* available hooks to build your competitive profile. Which of those factors *can* you change and *directly* control? Let's look at how the three hooks you directly control can help you build your profile as a competitive college applicant.

CHAPTER EIGHT

Understanding Your Hooks

Before we learn how to make these hooks work for you, let's take a helpful little quiz that will give you a realistic sense of your *relative* position in the applicant pool. The eight hooks used by competitive college admissions officers can intersect at multiple points and in multiple ways, so let's figure out where you stand in each of these categories and sharpen our approach to your application process.

The Eight-Factor Quiz

HOOKS YOU CAN'T CHANGE

1. Race

3 points if Black, Hispanic, Native American, Native Hawaiian

2 points if White

1 point if Asian

2. Geography

3 points if foreign (other than Chinese and Indian), from the Midwest or Mountain States, or from Alaska or Hawaii

2 points if from anywhere else (other than New York City, California, New Jersey, or Long Island)

1 point if from New York City, California, New Jersey, or Long Island

3. Legacy

3 points if *both* your parents attended your dream college

2 points if *either* parent attended your dream college

1 point if either or both parents attended a graduate program at your dream college

4. Citizenship/Nativity

3 points for being from an unusual country or being an undocumented immigrant, and achieving a 3-point status in two of the categories listed above

2 points for being a foreign citizen and getting 3 points in two of the categories listed above

1 point for being an American citizen

5. Family Income Level

3 points if your family income level is less than $65,000

2 points if your family income level is less than $150,000

1 point for all other family income levels

FACTORS YOU CAN CHANGE

1. Academics

3 points if combined SAT is 2300 or above and GPA is 4.0 or above

2 points if combined SAT is 2100 or above and GPA is 3.7 or above

1 point if combined SAT is lower than 2100 and GPA is below 3.7

2. Athletics

3 points if you are a nationally or internationally ranked individual athlete

2 points if you are on a nationally ranked or state championship team

1 point if you are on a varsity team that isn't nationally ranked or on the state championship level

3. Extracurriculars

3 points if you won any national or international competitions in your activity

2 points for extraordinary contributions genuinely validated or measured by an independent and credible source (e.g., research with an institution of higher education, state-level achievement)

1 point for all other levels of extracurricular activities

A maximum score is 24. But don't fret, perfection is more or less impossible on the Eight-Factor Quiz because you would have to look something like this: low income (3 points), Hispanic (3 points), foreign citizen (3 points), whose parents attended the target school (3 points) and had the foresight to send you to high school in Wyoming (3 points), where you achieved star academic status (3 points) and were a nationally ranked squash player (3 points), all while captaining the debate team to a national championship (3 points).

Most people will fall short of this. But it's quite possible that you are a mid-income (2 points) African American (3 points) from Denver (3 points) who is an exceptional skier (3 points), highly ranked academically (3 points), a gifted bassoonist in the state orchestra (2 points), with a parent who attended a graduate school at the target university (1 point), and an American citizen (1 point). This would make you an 18. It's a very high score and one that will ensure you'll get into an array of top-tier schools. In fact, any score above 14 (or 12 if you are Asian) puts you in a strong, competitive position.

If you score anything less than a 12, you'll need to increase your performance in those categories that you have the power to change. Scoring low in the "cannot change" categories means you need to work harder on the "can change" categories. (See the case studies of Michelle and Aaron later in the book.)

Once you've found your best fit, develop your hooks and talents while working to become a Combo or even a SuperCombo. You have a higher chance of success if you can identify the right story for yourself, one that accords with a college's need to fill the various groups.

A HOLISTIC VIEW ON FINDING YOUR BEST FIT

If you are guided by the "be the best you can be" mantra, you will find your fit and competitive advantage with relative ease and confidence. Focusing on a bigger purpose—your best self—will help you realize your best college fit, and allow you to take greater control of your life and academic future.

Finding your best fit—and then *being* your best fit—is a process based on personal growth, maturity, and introspection. Focus on the hooks you can control, accept those you cannot. Life is a delicate balance between seeking positive change and accepting your karma.

Personal Growth + Fit + Hook = Competitive Fit (Combo/SuperCombo)

We've looked at the five key hooks you *cannot* change and how they affect the construction of a college class. But what about the three hooks that you *can* change and over which you have direct control? I call these the Three A's.

1. Academics and Field of Study
2. Athletics
3. Activities

The Three A's are closely evaluated by admissions offices in relation to the specific slots they are trying fill. Competitive candidates—those who are outstanding in academics, athletics, or who have star talents in other activities—will rise to the tops of their baskets. In general, you're more likely to refine your fit by focusing on core strengths. Beware of the old adage "Jack of all trades and master of none." *Do not chase a multitude of activities and spread yourself too thin.* You are more likely to find your hook by going deep rather than wide.

Validations, awards, and honors provide external confirmation of your achievements and strengthen your hooks. Everyone is *not* a winner in the college admissions game; how the outside world perceives your talent is important, separating the Standard Strong from the outstanding. When an award or honor can reflect leadership skills—being elected class president, for instance—it is particularly alluring in the eyes of a college admissions officer. Given the increased competition and the global demand for an American university education, achievements are evaluated on a local, national, and even international level. So while a term as school president is an impressive achievement, Intel Science Prize winner is *more* impressive, and the exceptional, rare international validation of Olympic athlete would top all!

CHAPTER NINE

Academics

Outstanding Intellect

Most competitive colleges use something called the Academic Index (AI) to measure a student's competitive strength. Originally used to evaluate athletes, the AI is now employed as a universal tool for ranking students on the basis of grades, GPA (grade point average), or class rank and standardized tests. These scores are then aggregated and condensed into a single number. There is much speculation as to the relative weight accorded to each component of the AI, but it's generally agreed that a student's grades are the most important.

Competitive colleges want to see not only an impressive GPA, but also a high degree of difficulty in your course load. At most high schools, the competitive student will include several APs (advanced placement courses) in their course schedule. There are, of course, a number of factors taken into consideration at America's best colleges, but there will always be space for truly extraordinary intellects, Intel Science Competition winners, burgeoning research scientists, inventors, and entrepreneurs. These rare intellectual powerhouses go well beyond the AI markers of test scores and grades and course work to truly outpace the competition. For the rest of the pack, strong grades and brains alone are unlikely to be enough to place you beyond the Standard Strong category.

A WORD ABOUT HIGH SCHOOL COURSE LOAD

Strategically plan your high school course load. Your competitive position will be judged relative to the strength of your peers. Take the most challenging courses you can successfully handle. When choosing courses, consider that subjects like math, physics, and foreign languages will be viewed by colleges as indicators of genuine intellectual curiosity and academic talent.

Different high schools have different course offerings and systems. It's obviously not possible to directly compare course loads between different high schools—there are obvious differences, such as weighted vs. unweighted GPAs. Here are a few basic pieces of advice for assembling a high school curriculum that will be seen as academically rigorous and will immediately differentiate you as a serious student, capable of handling a competitive college curriculum.

Language: If you have an aptitude for foreign languages, take as many courses as possible, and at least four years of a modern or classical language. If possible, take more than one language.

Sciences: Take at least one full-year course in each of the three main sciences (biology, physics, and chemistry).

Math: Take math all four years of high school. For a competitive college application, you should aim to get through AP Calculus BC. At this level of math achievement you will also see a secondary benefit when taking standardized tests in math.

Special or Unusual Courses: Take courses that are out of the ordinary and challenging—astronomy or an unusual language like Chinese or Arabic. These classes will be seen as a differentiating, interesting supplement to your core curriculum. Note that these courses should be supplements (not replacements) to the basic high-level math and science courses.

How to Raise the Bar on Standardized Tests

Standardized tests form an important component of your application. With a few exceptions (notably Bowdoin, Hamilton, Bates, and Mount Holyoke), most competitive colleges require the SATs or ACTs. Since both tests are now perfectly acceptable, choose the one on which you are more likely to achieve a higher score. ACTs are considered less "tricky" in terms of how questions are posed, but require strong time-management skills. Students for whom English is not a first language must meet additional testing requirements, like TOEFFL or IELTS. Colleges look carefully at test scores, and high scores have the benefit of potentially earning you additional validations, like a National Merit Scholarship.

Your ability to score well on these tests is directly linked to the number of hours you have committed to taking practice tests, so manage your time carefully. You might have to take these tests more than once, so be disciplined. There is no substitute for methodical, regular practice when preparing for standardized tests. Last-minute cramming will not translate into a strong standardized test performance. If you doubt your ability to perform well on standardized tests or you have time-management issues, it is worth seeking test-preparation help. However, tutors are expensive and not a substitute for individual effort and practice. They may help structure your time and provide useful orientation, tips, and tricks, but they cannot do the work for you. You still need to spend the time and put in many hours of test preparation and practice.

Another factor that the admissions office considers is the expressed academic interests of the incoming class. If a school were to admit students out of proportion to what a particular department can handle, a major staff adjustment would be required

Fields of Study—Average Breakdown at Top Colleges

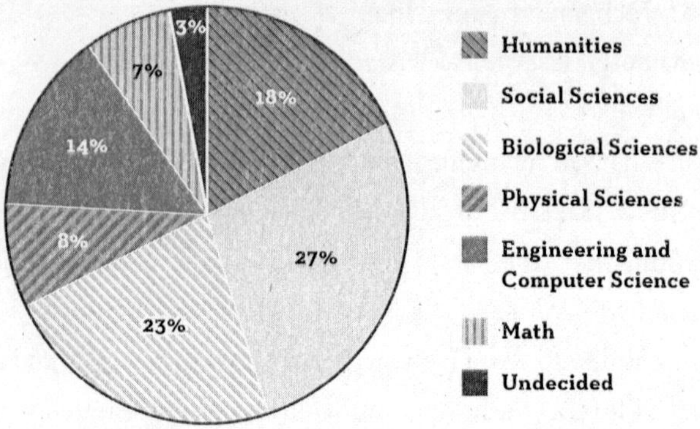

and, with widespread tenure, this is financially and practically impossible. Thus, there is a de facto pattern to the areas of study for which students are admitted. This may not be the first factor in determining admission, but it does play a role and can be used effectively by the applicant.

Reviewing data for field of study, on average 52 percent of an incoming Ivy League class opts for a "hard" science. There are important variations by college. Harvard, for example, reports the highest number of students opting for the humanities (25 percent), as opposed to 17 percent at Brown and only 12 percent at Dartmouth. The top fifteen chosen majors for Yale's 2017 incoming class in alphabetical order are as follows:

Biology
Biomedical engineering
Chemical engineering
Chemistry
Cognitive sciences
Economics
Economics and math
English
History
International studies
Math
Physics
Political science
Politics and economics
Psychology

Notably absent? Foreign languages, art history, and the classics.

When we combine this information with data about national degrees awarded by subject, we are left with what I call *Admissions Arbitrage by Field of Study*. The Admissions Arbitrage highlights academic fields where there is a *disproportionate* difference in the participation rate of men and women. If this difference is larger than a factor of three, there is a distinct need for additional males or females, as the case may be.

I have identified areas in the data offering clear Admissions Arbitrage opportunities. Some of these opportunities are in practical fields, such as accounting, which most competitive colleges eschew as not within their stated missions.

For instance, on a national basis, the recent gender breakdown of accounting majors was 4,934 males versus 15,245 females. In other words, *three times as many women* were pursuing associate degrees in accounting. Based on this data, a male applicant who expressed an interest in accounting would have a clear admissions advantage. Therefore, the advantage in accounting rates as a 3.0X Male Admissions Arbitrage.

A few other fields of study with strong arbitrages:

Fields of study in need of men

Accounting: 3X
Education: 6X
Foreign languages: 4X
Health careers: 6X (skewed by nursing)
Psychology: 3X
Social Services: 6X

Fields of study in need of women

Natural resources and conservation: 3X
Computer sciences: 3X
Engineering: 7X

It's not difficult to review the majors offered by your target college and then work out which are most likely to be heavily male- or female-dominated. At competitive colleges, Admissions Arbitrage opportunities include women opting for computer science or engineering and men pursuing obscure foreign languages and psychology.

There may also be similar opportunities presented by colleges themselves. Colleges are dynamic institutions with constantly changing priorities. Be aware of how a college's current admissions policy might affect your field of study hook. Describing Wesleyan's admissions process, journalist Jacques Steinberg writes that by 2002, the school's admissions committee was prioritizing qualified science students in an effort to balance the school's already strong liberal arts ethos. More recently, Harvard (along with other top colleges) has been paying close attention to the declining numbers of humanities students.

Remember, in most cases there is *absolutely nothing* that binds you to your professed major. Unlike most European or Asian systems, the American system allows for change and flexibility. No matter your expressed academic interest during the admissions process, you will be completely free to change your major once you have been admitted. At most top colleges, you won't even pick your major until your sophomore year, and by then the admissions office will have long forgotten about you.

It's important to develop a cogent story that reflects your interest in a field of study that is "against type." You could be that inner-city student who loves soccer, is fascinated by Brazilian soccer players, and wants to study Portuguese. It's a believable story—hopefully genuine—and worthy of exploration for a potential admissions hook.

ANTI-STEREOTYPING

Much has been written about the reverse discrimination faced by Asian American students and foreign students from China and India. I am not here to judge the fairness of the system but merely point out that if you are an Asian applicant, you will have to be roughly twice as good as the next Asian applicant—the 44 percent Asian American student population at Berkeley (no artificial cap) vs. the 20 percent at Harvard (possibly an unspoken limit on incoming Asian students) bearing that ratio out almost perfectly. Knowing this, an Asian applicant can make adjustments early in the process to stand out in the competitive pool of other Asians. Make no mistake, you are going to be judged against other Asian applicants, no matter what colleges say. I call this tactic "anti-stereotyping" and it can be extremely effective.

Anti-stereotyping is the process of turning perceived admissions weaknesses into strengths by modifying factors you cannot change with intelligent use of factors you can change. Fair or not, there are many broadly accepted stereotypes by gender, race, income level, citizenship—stereotypes that correspond to those five factors that you cannot change, though you can play with expectations in a way that will rebound to your benefit.

For example, a linebacker who weighs 250 pounds and has achieved All-State recognition in football is not expected to be an accomplished ballet dancer. If that linebacker were also to have starred in the high school production of *Swan Lake*, you can imagine the joy and recognition from admissions committees: "A linebacker who has also put his physical skills to use in the arts! Admit!"

This is anti-stereotyping at its best and it leads straight into a great *tagline*: "The dancing linebacker." Taglines are one-line candidate summations and they serve an important function in case evaluations. Assuming his academics are in the required range, the dancing linebacker will be an easy success story; he goes against type and his story is utterly memorable. Remember, admissions officers have to plough through upwards of 30,000 files. Catchy, descriptive taglines will help move your file to the top of the pile.

Anti-stereotypes like "debater who practices silent meditation" and "student who supplemented family income working at horse stables and rose to become a star polo player" are more common than you might think and are more memorable than the average, highly qualified Standard Strong candidate. Any version of these anti-stereotypes will be effective if pursued with commitment and zeal.

USING HIDDEN NETWORKS

Hidden networks exist all around us: in school, on the sports field, at extracurricular activities. Often these networks are hidden because they are only revealed or visible to those who deserve to benefit from them. An excellent example: the math teacher at your school who attended a top college and has remained in close touch with both that school's math department and admissions office. This teacher is possibly a valued talent spotter for that college. Because she uses her recommendations sparingly, reserving them for the occasional truly brilliant students she teaches, the math department at her college trusts her judgment. When a great student comes along, the teacher alerts the college's math department, who in turn alerts the admissions office, and the process of recruitment has begun. Such networks might not be visible to the naked eye, but they are ubiquitous. So be alert to those who are willing to use their connections and influence to assist your journey to one of America's top colleges.

CHAPTER TEN

Athletics

While colleges value all extraordinary talents, it's frequently athletes who enjoy favored status in college admissions. Sports are a time-honored route to collecting validations—independent confirmations of talent and achievement. *Leadership potential* is a buzzword in college admissions, and sporting success and winning are often equated with leadership. Colleges also value the supposed psychological advantage of successful sports programs, which they believe contribute to an atmosphere of optimism, camaraderie, and achievement. There is a strong feel-good factor associated with sporting success and this translates into feeling good about student athletes in the admissions process.

Athletes are needed to fill the large number of sports teams (which often provide colleges with significant revenue streams), making them an in-demand talent group. On average, top colleges field twenty-five sports teams, and recent National Collegiate Athletics Association (NCAA) statistics show that there are 420,000 athletes spread across 1,000 colleges. At the highest level, outstanding sporting achievement can lead to the Holy Grail status of the admissions process: the status of "recruited athlete."

RECRUITED ATHLETES

Outstanding high school athletes enjoy the ultimate hook as *recruited* athletes. These students are visible and easily identifiable, with colleges frequently pursuing and competing for them. As a result, recruited athletes (among non-Ivy League colleges) are bound by National Letters of Intent (NLIs), a binding agreement made by students to attend colleges offering them athletic scholarships.

Within the Ivy League, where scholarships are assessed on a need basis, the equivalent offer is the "likely letter." Likely letters are sent to student athletes identified by Ivy coaches for their sporting excellence and who are also deemed academically qualified by admissions officers. However, likely letters are not binding. The actual admissions process and balance between sporting vs. academic ability varies from "generous" for big-ticket sports to "moderate" for niche sports. Ivy admissions officers often refer to the "break-a-leg rule"—if the athlete is felled by an injury, could they remain on campus purely as a student?—to ensure minimum academic standards are met.

In either case, it's the student athlete who has the upper hand and is in solid control of the process. Whether it is an NLI or a "likely letter" at an Ivy, the student has a valuable admissions slot (or promise) months before other applicants even mail their applications.

So how favored are college-bound athletes?

It's an answer that involves approximation because it's difficult to assess how many athletes wouldn't be admitted on a purely academic admissions standard. Athletes are often excellent time-managers and many have also compiled strong academic records. Often, these student athletes are capable multitaskers as Combos (even SuperCombos) and objectively fit the profile of competitive college applicants.

Using our model class of 1,600 students, we estimate approximately 400 admitted athletes—or almost one-quarter of the class. Taking a high estimate, let's assume that half of these athletes are academically underqualified. That's almost 200 slots for athletes who otherwise might not "deserve" to be there. And that's a full 12.5 percent of the class and by far the largest group of candidates

SuperCombo—A Winning Combination

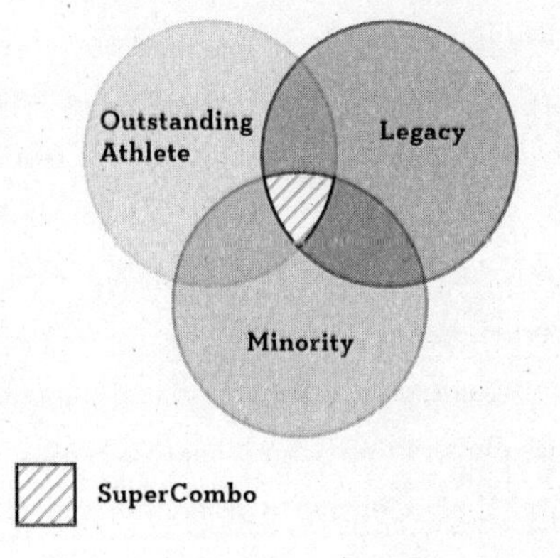

who might not be admitted otherwise. An analysis of this 12.5 percent number is far more complicated, of course, as athletes tend to overlap with legacies and minorities. A high proportion of legacies too are top athletes, likely because they have been raised in families wealthy enough to underwrite and encourage niche sports like rowing, fencing, squash, skiing, and golf.

Ivy League colleges have the finances to field a large number of sports teams and athletes (those qualified to play on a varsity-level team in intercollegiate sports) make up about 20 percent of the student body. While Ivy League colleges recruit athletes, they are technically barred from offering sports scholarships. Since a number of Ivy schools have need-blind admissions policies, which do not take into account an applicant's ability to pay, sports scholarships are often disguised as need-based scholarships, available to lower income athletes but not to higher income athletes. For athletes from high-income families, this matters little, but there is a breaking point at which it matters very much, hitting the middle-class applicant hardest.

If you are just rich enough not to qualify for financial aid, but not so rich that the $65,000-per-year cost of a top college isn't a financial burden, you may wish to look at colleges that offer straight sports scholarships. In fact, athletic scholarships often lure athletes away from the Ivy League and toward less competitive colleges. Journalist Daniel Golden also observes that "Ivy League schools often recruit more players than they need to fill rosters, anticipating that, without a financial incentive to play, some will quit their sport."

Popular Ivy sports like crew also have high injury and attrition rates and therefore depend on a large pool of recruited athletes. And specific colleges favor specific sports—squash has long been a favorite among the Ivy League colleges, Notre Dame has a long tradition of competitive fencing, and Duke is famously associated with basketball.

Since the Ivy League is barred from offering athletic scholarships and must balance athletic desirability with academic ability, it's not easy for colleges to fill their rosters, particularly for niche sports where the recruiting policy is not as determinative as in the big-money sports of football and basketball. Competitive colleges impose more exacting academic standards, though these vary both within Ivy League colleges and among different sports.

Given the recruiting constraints faced by the Ivy League, there is a real opportunity for an outstanding student athlete to wrest control of the Ivy admissions process. This is true especially for outstanding athletes who don't require financial aid. Many of these are rich white students who play the so-called country club sports, generally requiring expensive equipment or facilities (think fencing, golf, water polo, skiing, squash, and tennis).

It is frequently argued that the focus on squash, tennis, skiing, and golf is a backdoor way of favoring legacy children and wealthy, foreign students who have greater access to such sports. By the same token, if you are from a low-income family and are a talented athlete, you could enjoy an even greater advantage. If you fit the recruited athlete profile, congratulations! You just may have written your own ticket into a top college! Outstanding success in any sport requires hours of dedication and practice, so quite apart from the "favored applicant" status this will earn you, you'll also accrue points for your hard work and time-management skills.

Competition Is Good—Enjoy It

This opportunity for talented student athlete Combos has not gone unnoticed. Competitive students have flocked toward niche sports such as squash, fencing, and water polo, driving up standards and performance to near professional levels. It's important to mention that performance (not mere participation) is the driving force behind the outstanding athlete hook. With performance levels progressing to new highs, recruited athletes now need to excel on a national and international level to attract a coach's attention.

In our discussion of how a college constructs a class, we presented an example where multiple filters can help to analyze your position in the college landscape. By applying these filters, we see, for instance, that if you are an Asian American woman from the Midwest there will likely be approximately fifteen of your type admitted. Are you among the fifteen best candidates in this basket—female, Asian American, from the Midwest? If so, you have a clear chance. If you think you are in the top 100 of this group, you should apply because your odds would be pretty good at about 1 in 7.

To maximize your chance of admission as a female, Asian American, Midwestern student, you'll need to be a top applicant from this subgroup. You manage this by focusing on hooks you can change, such as academic and extracurricular-activity achievement. And there are probably ways for you to analyze this, from Midwestern regional school groups, cultural activity groups, or sports leagues where you can judge yourself against your competition.

CASE STUDY: Michelle from Orange, New Jersey

Type: Asian—Northeast—US Citizen—Middle Income

Background: Michelle was a high-achieving, disciplined, competitive student entering a local public high school. She had excellent grades and strong extracurriculars, particularly in community service, where she organized several fundraising initiatives to support her community work. She was first-generation American, brought up by parents who firmly believed in top grades and academic achievement as a means to realizing the American dream. For Michelle and her parents, a further realization of this dream was attendance at an Ivy League university. Michelle was aware of the Ivy dream before most of her non-Asian friends could read.

Challenge: Michelle lived in a predominantly Asian community. Culturally, there was a common thread running through most families—work hard and perform at the top of the class. While Michelle lived up to these expectations, so did her many Asian American friends. As Michelle approached the all-important high school years, the problem was how to differentiate herself from this very accomplished, competitive basket of Asian Americans in Orange, New Jersey. What was her unique hook?

Plan of Action: As a child, Michelle was in awe of her namesake, champion figure skater Michelle Kwan. Along with many of her Korean friends, she had started skating early and grew up with the discipline of a rigorous practice schedule. Michelle was a solid skater but clearly not destined to follow in the footsteps of her heroine. Was it possible to take the discipline, strength, stamina, and coordination she had gained from skating and translate it into greater success in another sport?

Michelle was nurtured with a "can-do, work hard" ethic. And before long, she began fencing. An only child, she had the full support of her parents, who always packed a picnic basket and drove her to local clubs and competitions. She trained hard, hung on her coach's every word, and then practiced her footwork (already limber from the rigors of skating) in her spare time. What she lacked in natural talent she made up for in sheer determination and work ethic. By ninth grade, her first year of high school, Michelle began to win. She won club competitions and then community tournaments. Competitive fencing was still a relatively small sport, and, relying on her natural competitive spirit and tactical mind, Michelle made rapid progress.

By the end of ninth grade, she was competing at state level. By tenth grade, she had a national ranking and was competing in national competitions. Whether in Atlanta or Boston, her parents were right there with her. By eleventh grade, Michelle was regularly ranked in the top eight fencers nationally. And while she lacked the natural talent to propel her to Olympic-level fencing, her consistency in a small, niche sport was sufficient to secure a single-digit national ranking.

Solution: By taking a strategic decision to move from skating to the niche sport of fencing, Michelle succeeded in differentiating herself from her Asian American peers and refining her fit from Standard Strong Asian American to a Combo or competitive fit as nationally ranked student athlete Asian American. She moved to the top of one of the most competitive baskets in the admissions process and made herself visible to Ivy league fencing coaches charged with the daunting task of finding accomplished fencers who were also strong students.

Result: Michelle was recruited by an Ivy League college. She received a likely letter in September and was formally admitted in November.

CHAPTER ELEVEN

Extracurricular Activities

Following the pattern of superstar athlete or intellectual, this category includes exceptional ability in the arts (music, dance, drama, letters) or activities (community leadership, politics, or social activism). It's not enough to rush off on prescription travel adventures like Rustic Pathways or play violin in a school orchestra. Outstanding talents have played Carnegie Hall, been on (or just Off-) Broadway, and published original work. They have spent years effecting meaningful change in the inner city or remote rural communities. They collect genuine validations and are student leaders.

CASE STUDY: Aaron from Greenwich, Connecticut

TYPE: White—Northeast—Legacy—US Citizen—High Income

Background: Aaron was a typical Standard Strong candidate. He never got below an A in any high school course and graduated with a 4.1 GPA. His SAT I and II scores were well over 700. He had excellent recommendations from key teachers at his prestigious, well-respected private school in the wealthy enclave of Greenwich, Connecticut. He was involved in an impressive array of extracurricular activities: student government member, player on a midranked lacrosse team, Model United Nations delegate, student drama contributor, and volunteer at a soup kitchen in a nearby town. His parents both attended Yale, but Aaron prioritized getting away from Connecticut, which he found stifling. He had his heart set on Stanford, due to its reputation as a feeder to Silicon Valley, despite knowing little about computer programming.

Challenge: How would Aaron overcome the fact that his background, while strong, looked very similar to the background of about 50 percent of Stanford applicants?

Aaron's parents were both Ivy League graduates who kept themselves well apprised of the admissions process. Back when Aaron was a high school freshman, they knew their son suffered from "suburban sameness" and understood the volume of applicants who looked very much like their son. And they were aware that top colleges could fill their classes many times over with versions of Aaron. By Aaron's sophomore year, his Standard Strong profile was apparent: He performed close to, but not quite at, the very top level. His parents later realized that had Aaron attended the town's highly rated—and free—

public high school, he would have looked every bit as competitive, possibly more so. His Standard Strong background was expected, coming from an elite Northeast private high school. His parents saw that he was bounding toward an *almost* top college but not *quite* a top college. They had ambitions for Aaron and money was no object, so they hired a well-known college admissions consultant when Aaron was entering tenth grade.

Plan of Action: After interviewing Aaron, the admissions consultant immediately grasped the problem. Aaron lacked a passion. Sure, he was smart enough to achieve at a high level in almost every subject, but he was not *inspired* enough to find something in which he could truly stand out. It was a common problem among privileged students: They shifted into a gear in which they could coast (admittedly a high gear, due to their natural advantages and inputs), but failed to accelerate to become well positioned for a top-ranked college. Aaron needed to find an area in which he had a genuine interest. Making up an interest, the consultant advised, would seem transparent. Aaron's father was politically conservative, donating to causes and candidates that Aaron found antithetical to his own nascent political views. Although the consultant knew it was a risky strategy, she sensed in him a budding political activist. She saw the opportunity in anti-stereotyping: Aaron engaging actively in liberal politics could counteract his privileged status; disagreeing politically with his father but learning to respect their differences could bring them closer in the process.

Solution: The consultant encouraged Aaron to engage his budding interest in politics. Together they checked election schedules, noting an upcoming Senate election in Connecticut and mapping out a strategy for getting involved in local Democratic Party politics. It turned out that his father had gone to college with the Democratic Senate candidate's campaign manager and, although it hurt him to see Aaron in the opposing political camp, he wrangled an introduction for his son. Soon Aaron was spending ten to fifteen hours a week on the campaign. By the time college application season rolled around, Aaron was head of the candidate's youth volunteer group, appearing at events around the state and even supervising volunteers from local colleges. By the time the candidate won in November—just in time for Aaron to send his application to California—Aaron was a confident and accomplished public speaker, a motivated young man, and perhaps a future candidate himself.

Result: Aaron was admitted to Stanford. A letter of recommendation from a newly elected United States senator certainly helped his case. But Aaron had also applied to Yale, after having worked on its campus during the campaign and feeling at home there. The following year Aaron found himself scouting opportunities to run for local office—in New Haven.

CHAPTER TWELVE

Using Your Hooks

Students with outstanding talents in the Three A's should use these hooks to maximum advantage. Let's turn back to the five hooks you cannot change and see how these can be *selectively used* to your advantage. Unlike the talent hooks (the Three A's) that are available to all students, the five hooks you cannot change can only be used by—or are only accessible to—a select group of students. Factors such as legacy and diversity aren't universally applicable and say less about a student's achievement than about their family or circumstances. For example, favored minorities or Standard Strong students who also happen to be legacies will become more competitive as Combos or even Super-Combos. Life is not, alas, a level playing field, and if you choose to play the competitive college game, you have to accept what you cannot change.

Diversity

A diversity hook is most effective as a supplement to an already strong candidate. A diversity hook can move a student into the intersection of our Venn diagram illustrations. There is room for students to be proactive and make their diversity hook work for them.

LIVING UP TO YOUR STEREOTYPE

Just as we spoke about anti-stereotyping, there are times when you should fully *embrace* stereotypes. This is most true if you are a member of a favored minority group. African American, Hispanic, and Native American students should seek out activities that bear out the true vitality of their culture and identity. Embracing your identity is part of the journey to finding your best self. If you think you are "too white" to qualify as culturally interesting, dig deep and look more carefully at your background. Start with your grandparents. Was grandpa Albanian? Is there an Albanian heritage society in your area? You can start reading up on Albania and exploring a distant part of the world with which you have hitherto been unconnected. With some reflection, introspection, and genuine inclination, you can create an interesting cultural story even without being part of an "obvious" minority.

CASE STUDY: Joaquin from Los Angeles

Type: Hispanic–West–US Citizen–Low-Income

Background: Joaquin was born and raised in a working-class neighborhood in East Los Angeles. His parents were undocumented Mexican immigrants at the time of Joaquin's birth. Because he was born in the United States, Joaquin was a citizen, though his parents remained undocumented until he was in high school, when they were naturalized. His father was a skilled mechanic; his mother worked in various garment factories that dotted downtown Los Angeles. Neither of Joaquin's parents had graduated from high school, but they were both literate and his father possessed a deep love of reading and music. His mother was religious and a regular visitor to their local Catholic church. Joaquin demonstrated a high level of intelligence at an early age, and his church's clergy took notice. One of the priests arranged to have Joaquin attend the best Jesuit high school in Los Angeles, where he received a high-quality education and from which a large percentage of students went on to college, especially within the California state system.

Challenge: While Joaquin was among the best students at his high school and capable of handling the academic rigor at a top college, he simply did not have access to the college world outside his home state of California. It was easy for him to follow the well-worn path of talented students at his school and end up at one of California's state campuses where in-state tuition was affordable. Joaquin's challenge was even more difficult because neither of his parents had any idea about college, let alone college outside California. Indeed, they effectively had no input at all in his college application process.

Plan of Action: Joaquin was on a path to attend California State Fullerton, which had a large Hispanic population. But his guidance counselor, Father Hernan, believed strongly in his ability, seeing a student with strong academic and musical abilities who had overcome several socioeconomic hurdles. When Father Hernan became Joaquin's mentor and took a keen interest in his college application process, he called several admissions offices at top colleges across the country and spoke repeatedly with the relevant admissions officers. He knew it was difficult for these colleges to find qualified Hispanic applicants—especially from East Los Angeles who were willing to attend college on the other side of the country. Father Hernan made an impassioned case for Joaquin, detailing his background and explaining why he was a special candidate. He also connected Joaquin with a high school alumnus who was currently a senior at an Ivy League college.

Solution: With the help, guidance, and determination of Father Hernan, Joaquin was able to maintain regular contact with five competitive East Coast colleges. Personal meetings with admissions officers from three of these colleges were arranged while on their regular recruiting trips to Los Angeles. A number of interested admissions officers were now eyeing Joaquin as a candidate capable of occupying a special category that they often had difficulty filling.

Joaquin was articulate, engaging, funny, and wise beyond his years. His life story was deeply impressive. He was also a strong student and talented musician, having been taught to play Mexican folk music on the guitar by his father. All of this impressed the admissions officers, but his story and personality might not have come across as effectively if they were based solely on his academic record and application, no matter how well rendered. Each officer who met Joaquin encouraged him to apply to their competitive college; it was advice he was happy to take. The common application made the process of multiple applications relatively easy. And he was also able to get an application fee waiver from all the colleges to which he applied, saving him hundreds of dollars. Both Father Hernan and his school's alumnus provided valuable help and guidance with his application.

Result: Joaquin was admitted to a top Ivy League college (the same college attended by his school's alumnus) with a full financial-aid package. Apart from the backing of his mentor, his personal interviewer wrote an enthusiastic recommendation that further enhanced his competitive fit. He was also admitted to two other top (non-Ivy) colleges and to California State Northridge. Joaquin accepted his Ivy League offer.

Postscript: Joaquin did well enough at his Ivy to graduate in the middle of the class. He was the first in his family to earn a college degree and would later go on to attend UCLA School of Law.

He practices law and lives in West Los Angeles.

DIVERSITY AND COMMUNITY SERVICE

Leadership is a buzzword often employed when discussing college admissions. And for those not athletically inclined and unlikely to be the captain of the football team, community service offers an opportunity to be a leader. Some of the most powerful stories in both life and on college applications are from minority or disadvantaged students volunteering and helping others in their communities.

In America, *community* is often defined rather narrowly as your immediate ethnic group and rarely as your class group. If a Hispanic student from the inner city were to invest time and effort volunteering with poor Hmong refugees, it would no doubt be worthy of accolades but would also seem somewhat discordant to many college admissions officers. In general, America expects a Hispanic community activist to be involved with the Hispanic community. There is a subtle racism at work here, where minorities are expected to be most active in helping out "their" group, while white students (who are generally better off) can freely volunteer in Myanmar because their nonminority status allows them the freedom to volunteer with any ethnic or racial group. That said, a Hmong student from inner-city Minneapolis who volunteers at a Hmong social center is exactly what colleges expect—and celebrate in an applicant.

Gender and Sexual Diversity

Society's definition and views of gender and sexual identity have shifted significantly in recent years, with colleges quickly reconsidering and redefining these important cultural categories. For instance, sexual diversity, previously only identified with gay applicants, now includes children raised by gay parents. Most college campuses are liberal enclaves where this type of diversity is celebrated.

So as students search for hooks in an ever more competitive process, they can use sexual diversity as a way of differentiating themselves. Often, gender identity and sexual orientation are reflected in a student's choice of extracurricular activities and it could be useful to reflect these traits in parts of the application process, notably the college essay. For instance, a touching coming-out story could be seen as brave, unique, or self-aware. But as with every aspect of the process, *do not depict yourself as something you are not.* Also, while the admissions process is confidential, we do not suggest that the first place you confide something very private about your sexuality is in your admissions essay. However, if you genuinely feel that you can use this diversity hook, consider doing so.

CASE STUDY: Oliver from Dallas

Type: White—South—US Citizen—Mid-Income

Background: Oliver was universally liked at his competitive private school. Quiet but popular, he was a sensitive, gentle, conscientious young man. His grades and academic work placed him in the top 5 percent of his class. He was a talented musician, principal cellist in the school's orchestra, and his community-service work involved teaching music to local public school children, largely migrants from Mexico.

Challenge: With his solid lineup of academic and extracurricular accomplishments, Oliver was very much a Standard Strong applicant. With his heart set on an Ivy League college, how was he going to find an added hook to lift his competitive fit from Standard Strong to admit?

Plan of Action: By the end of his junior year, Oliver had consolidated his position as a high achiever. He was popular among students and staff alike and his quiet ambition set him apart from the rowdier guys in his class. However, he wondered if his excellent school record and musical accomplishments would be enough to create a truly unique college application. Oliver was well aware of the competition for spots in the Ivy League. As the hot Texas summer months melted into each other, he began to think about his application and how he could seize this opportunity to lift himself from a Standard Strong candidate to a *uniquely* strong candidate.

He had accomplished much in his academic and extracurricular life and come far in his personal life. But he had always felt different from most boys and men around him. As a child, he was drawn toward more typically feminine pursuits. He felt supported and nurtured by his family, but could not yet confront his feelings and doubts about his sexuality. Texas was a conservative state and his private school reflected the values of his surroundings. It wasn't that Oliver felt the need to conform, but he was unable to truly express who he felt he was.

Ninth grade was a turning point. Fritz, a fellow student, was elegant and slim, and he struck Ollie to the core, jolting him out of years of doubt. Oliver knew he was in love and was acknowledging that he was gay. He remembered his relief and joy at coming out. His newfound comfort and personal equilibrium, triggered by his coming out, had advantages in other areas as well. He was able to support other young musicians struggling with gender and sexuality issues, and he worked toward increasing awareness of sex education through his community work at public schools. With great controversy, he founded his school's first LGBT club. As he reflected on his personal journey, Oliver knew he had found a unique angle for the college essay he wanted to write.

Solution: A gifted writer, Oliver was able to craft that unique application essay—a coming-out story that, in turn, had a positive effect on other gay members of his community. He told his own unique story, revealing his struggles and fears, his integrity and perseverance, his courage, and his ultimate position of happiness and fulfillment. He successfully turned his initial fears into positive actions and was able to serve both his own interests and those of the wider gay community.

As it happened, his story fit closely with the listed common application essay topics. His essay packed an emotional punch and struck a unique note, combining sensitivity, positivity, and empowerment. In addition, Oliver was able to add the diversity factor to his already Standard Strong application. He was now a powerful Combo: academic, gay, musician, activist, and community worker from Texas!

Result: Oliver was admitted to two top Ivies, both on his dream college list.

Legacy

Connected Legacies can gain significant advantages in the admissions process. There are cases where medium and low achievers gain admission based on their family connections. While this is unfair, it is often most unfair in areas that are not immediately obvious: to the young students themselves. Pushing a young person outside their natural comfort zone can damage self-esteem, learning, and ability to navigate life successfully. Contrary to our belief that it's you who should be in control, the Connected Legacy hook leaves a student with little control over an important process. Do not be that square peg trying to force yourself into a round hole! It's when you have correctly judged your fit that your chances of success in the admissions process *and* as an admitted student are strongest.

CASE STUDY: Olivia from New York City

Type: White–Northeast–Legacy–US Citizen–High-Income

Background: Olivia's dad was determined that she attend his Ivy League alma mater. He had been a generous alumni donor even before his children were born. As wealthy New Yorkers, Olivia and her siblings attended the most desirable private schools and often spent weekends at a family retreat less than two hours away. Having access to a first-class education and any extracurricular diversion of her choice, Olivia benefited from a stimulating—and affluent—life. She did well enough in school, but was lost in the "great middle" of well-informed, articulate, young New Yorkers. She didn't shine in any area. She tried her hand at several extracurricular activities, finally settling on theater and field hockey. She was a member of the varsity field hockey team, but rarely started. She was involved with school theater, but typically as a technical assistant. Her grades were above average although not stellar—she earned a 3.6 GPA—but her father felt she was destined to attend his highly competitive alma mater.

Challenge: How could Olivia's father ensure his well educated, privileged (but ultimately high-average) daughter be admitted to a highly competitive Ivy League college?

Plan of Action: Olivia's dad was aware that he needed to play the "legacy hook" game. He understood the system, was clear on his priorities, and had considerable financial resources at his disposal. He had always been a generous donor and understood that the significance of his gifts would be a critical factor in his daughter's application process. As Olivia approached high school, his giving increased into "leadership" circles (defined at most competitive colleges as higher than $1 million). He also increased his volunteer time with the university, assuming an active role in fundraising activities. Generous donors are typically invited to sit on various university committees; he was active on several and took advantage of this in order to be known to those working with both the development office and admissions office. His picture appeared in the monthly college magazine in an article celebrating the school's most generous alumni donors.

He made it clear that Olivia must maintain her respectable GPA (above the class average) and continue with her extracurricular activities, showing commitment despite her only slightly above-average achievement. In addition, Olivia would have the best test preparation tutoring, her father having booked her a series of sessions with a sought-after instructor.

Solution: After a heavy tutoring schedule and a few attempts at the SAT, Olivia ultimately scored in the low 700s on all her tests. With additional private instruction, she increased her GPA to 3.7 at her highly competitive school. She managed to push her academic fit into Standard Strong. She retained her position on the field hockey team while adding an assistant director credit to her theater work at school. Her extracurriculars, although unremarkable, at least showed consistency.

When the time came to apply, her father was a major donor and a cochair of his class's 25th reunion.

Result: Once again, Olivia got her wish. Her father also realized his dream. Olivia was admitted to her father's alma mater. He had worked the Connected Legacy hook perfectly, pushing her from respectable fit into an admit. Olivia applied at a time when her father's college had briefly ceased offering the early-action option. She had no other Ivy League acceptances but was admitted to Georgetown. The legacy world is a protective tree, but it needs care and feeding to protect those it shelters.

Postscript: At college, the chickens came home to roost, but it didn't matter. Olivia did not challenge herself academically and maintained a B average, graduating in the middle of the class. She was unable to compete as a field hockey player but continued to assist on the technical side of college theater productions. She lives in New York City, working in public relations.

We have discussed eight hooks that determine your competitive advantage and affect the outcome of your college admissions process. The Three A's (academics, athletics, and extracurricular activities) are the hooks you can control directly, while the remaining five (race, geography, legacy, citizenship/nativity, and family income level) you cannot change but can use to your advantage. So use all legitimate hooks available to you to strengthen your competitive fit and start thinking about which college is right for you.

CHAPTER THIRTEEN

Choosing the Right College

You have embraced what fate and nature have tossed your way, seen the value in hard work, identified your hooks, and refined your fit. You have matured into a competitive fit—possibly even a Combo or SuperCombo.

So how does all of this translate into finding the right college for *you*?

As the details of your competitive fit become more clear, so will the process of finding the right college. I previously illustrated this point with the example of recruited athletes. When you can choose among colleges competing for your attention, you're in control and are consequently more likely to make the right choice. All top colleges similarly identify their top candidates. If you are fortunate to be among the best, you're likely to have multiple offers from top-tier schools. This places you in an enviable "no lose" position, increasing the likelihood that you will make a calm, wise, and objective choice when deciding which college is right for you. Your process becomes less about where you fit into the college landscape and more about which college best suits you.

Remember our holistic approach: Your long-term interests depend almost entirely on your appropriate fit. You want to be the peg that fits smoothly into your slot. If you have correctly identified your fit, your chances of being admitted to your dream college increase—as do your chances of a successful college experience. And all of this has the benefit of contributing to a more positive life.

Personal Growth → Fit → Competitive Fit → Right College

So which college is right for you?

Most students are neither recruited athletes nor do they possess other outstanding talents. While their hooks may not be as powerful, the general principle of seeking greater competitive advantage and control still applies. There are strategic decisions that might make a student more desirable to a particular college.

For all college-bound students, finding the right college involves careful research and planning. Look for colleges that favor your particular hook or interests. Understand the particular nuances of different colleges and how they might complement your fit. A budding scientist with top-level academics? Include MIT and Caltech on your list. A liberal arts enthusiast who would like to design your own curriculum? Include Brown and Wesleyan. Are you a talented fencer looking for a sports scholarship? Try Notre Dame, for its tradition and strength in fencing. If gender and sexual diversity are priorities, a top women's college might be your answer.

Go deep with researching colleges that match your interests, academic inclinations, and competitive advantage. Supplement your research by talking to people who understand you and are familiar with the competitive college environment. Network with current and former students, do extensive online research, and make connections that can help in refining your knowledge of particular colleges and the admissions process.

A WORD OF CAUTION

As the admissions process has become increasingly more competitive, so has the pressure on applicants to widen their admissions strategy by applying to upwards of a dozen colleges. College visits have become complex itineraries involving months of planning, expense, and stress. Do not get caught in this web. Be introspective and shut out the noise—and do what you can to resist this pressure and maintain control of your process. Under no circumstances should you let the process control you.

I believe that a college list including between eight and ten colleges, sensibly spread between reach, solid, and safety schools, is ideal. There is a breaking point beyond which nerves, paperwork, and ultimately the quality of your application will spiral out of control.

What about costly and time-consuming college visits? Do not do them at the early, option-creating stage of the application process. Postpone college visits until you have admissions acceptances in hand and are in the decision-making stage. While the admissions evaluation process itself has changed little over the years, application numbers and qualifications have soared. With most colleges in their competitive group (as defined below) basically similar in terms of "brand value," your goal is to be admitted by one or more colleges in the group best suited to your skills and abilities. In the option-creating stage, what particular college you are admitted to within the appropriate group is almost secondary. Your primary focus should be on considering your best chances within a *group* vs. at any particular college that might not be the appropriate fit.

Do you really need to join the overbooked tours marveling at Yale's gothic architecture? Do you really need to be distracted by figuring out which college has the most recently renovated dorms or the best breakfast? Do you really need to visit if your choice is between Princeton and Johns Hopkins? Probably not. I suggest that you consider postponing college visits until you are deciding between two (or more) schools within the highest group to which you are admitted. So if your choice is between Johns Hopkins and Georgetown, and you have offers in hand from each, certainly plan a decision-making visit. Only then can you make your decision based on who has the nicest dorms or the best breakfast.

College visits at the option-creating stage aren't particularly useful. In fact, they can harm the holistic process by threatening internal introspection with external noise. To allocate valuable resources to the tedious process of revealing slight differences between Carleton and Vassar (or even between Harvard and Yale) *before* you are admitted to each one is simply not the best use of your time, energy, and money.

At this stage, I recommend spending your time and resources on fine-tuning your achievements during your all-important—and busy—junior year.

That said, there are a few exceptions where initial-stage college visits are advisable.

If you benefit from a powerful hook and are confident in your unique ability to control the admissions process, it might be advisable—even necessary—to plan a college visit. We have described the unique position enjoyed by recruited athletes and other outstanding talents or favored minorities who might enjoy similar advantages. For these select students, early college visits are advisable—even more so when arranged by colleges actively seeking you.

These recruited students are on a different timeline and have the luxury of choosing between competitive, equivalent offers. For these students, getting an early sense or gut feeling about a college is relevant, even necessary, as they may be required to make early decisions and commit to colleges that have expressed an interest in them. Recruited athletes, for example, often have to commit to a college before the early application timeline. It is also important for these students to meet potential mentors—be it a college coach or a professor—who will likely influence a significant part of their college experience.

Should You Go to a Small College or a Large University?

1. What kind of coffee shop do you prefer?

Don't care. Anywhere with coffee	3 points
Starbucks	2 points
A local, neighborhood coffee shop	1 point

2. Where do you like to study?

School library	3 points
At Starbucks	2 points
In a cozy corner of my room	1 point

3. How do you like to get around?

Subway or bus	3 points
Car	2 points
Walk	1 point

4. Which type of sporting event would you rather watch?

Football	3 points
Track and field	2 points
Ultimate Frisbee	1 point

5. Which activity sounds most interesting to you?

Marching band	3 points
Community service	2 points
Knitting club	1 point

6. How well do you like to get to know your friends?

Just enough to be friends	3 points
Well enough to share confidences	2 points
Well enough to meet their parents	1 point

7. How do you refer to your teacher?

"That person way down in the front"	3 points
"Professor Jones"	2 points
"Bob"	1 point

8. The most people I am comfortable sharing a bathroom with is

Five	3 points
Two	2 points
None	1 point

- If you scored higher than 18, you would fit best at a large university.
- A score between 10 and 17 means that any size institution would work for you.
- If you scored below 10, your fit is much more likely to be a small liberal arts college.

- If you can decide between a small college and a large university, you'll immediately narrow down your choices by about half, simplify your process, and reduce stress.

The Top 50

We divide your options into two types of institutions: universities (larger) and colleges (smaller). We're looking only at the top fifty schools in each category and will further break down the top universities and top colleges into subcategories, or brands, coming up with four lists that reflect the generally accepted ranking data combined with my own subjective judgment and experience.

The True Top
The Next Best
The Solid Middle
The Rest

We specifically remove from these groupings all special-case schools, like military academies, music schools, and unusual, subsidized schools. While these schools serve particular functions in society (as discussed in more detail below), they are very different from the "normal" colleges and it makes little sense to compare them with mainstream institutions.

There is no point in ranking *within* these groups. The schools in each group are certainly not interchangeable, but they are broadly similar in terms of "brand value," particularly within the

Solid Middle and Rest categories. With notable exceptions, it's difficult to claim that someone who attended Bates will benefit from greater brand value and alumni connectivity or do appreciably better in life than someone who attended nearby Colby. However, the odds are good that a Stanford graduate will benefit from a higher valued brand than a graduate from either Bates or Colby.

We can define the value of a school's brand as what future benefits—largely socioeconomic and including future employment prospects—one can expect from your degree, based on the power of a college's reputation, visibility, and alumni networks.

So how are my rankings calculated? I created the list through careful analysis of the generally accepted ranking lists (*US News & World Report,* for instance) and college acceptance rates and yield statistics. I have also factored in a subjective judgment as to the value of certain university names as brands in the job market and professional world.

Note that for smaller colleges, we have combined the Next Best and Solid Middle, as it's almost impossible to make fine brand distinctions among these two groups.

UNIVERSITIES

The Best

Caltech
Harvard
MIT

Princeton

Stanford

Yale

The Next Best

Brown

Columbia

Cornell

Dartmouth

University of Chicago

University of Pennsylvania

The Solid Middle

Carnegie Mellon

Duke

Georgetown

Johns Hopkins

Northwestern

NYU

Rice

University of California, Los Angeles

University of California, Berkeley

University of Michigan, Ann Arbor

University of Southern California

University of Virginia

Vanderbilt

Washington University

The Rest

Boston College

Boston University

Brandeis

Case Western Reserve

College of William & Mary

Emory

Lehigh

Northeastern University

Notre Dame

Penn State

Rensselaer Polytechnic

Tufts

Tulane

University of California Davis

University of California, Irvine

University of California San Diego

University of California Santa Barbara

University of Illinois, Urbana-Champaign

University of Miami

University of North Carolina, Chapel Hill

University of Rochester

University of Wisconsin, Madison

Wake Forest

Yeshiva University

COLLEGES

The Best

Amherst

Bowdoin

Middlebury

Pomona

Swarthmore

Williams

The Next Best and the Solid Middle

Bates

Bryn Mawr

Carleton

Claremont

Colby

Colgate

Davidson

Grinnell

Hamilton

Harvey Mudd

Haverford

Mount Holyoke

Pitzer

Scripps

Smith

Trinity

Vassar

Washington & Lee

Wellesley

Wesleyan

The Rest

Bard

Barnard

Bucknell

Centre

Colorado College

Connecticut College

Denison

Dickinson

Franklin & Marshall

Gettysburg

Holy Cross

Kenyon

Lafayette

Macalester

Oberlin

Occidental

Sewanee

Skidmore

Union College

University of Richmond

Whitman

SPECIAL AND UNUSUAL INSTITUTIONS

The United States has several amazing educational institutions offering free tuition. But nothing is ever free and there is, of course, a pretty big caveat: Upon graduation, students must commit to a period of military service.

If you're applying to one of these institutions—West Point, Air Force Academy, Annapolis, The Merchant Marine Academy, The Coast Guard Academy—make sure you're thinking long-term. You'll be getting a great education, but you're also making a life choice that necessitates years of military service.

These institutions are very competitive and offer an education on par with the best colleges in the country. Entry is selective and competitive and you'll have to be a special candidate to get in and to graduate. We also include in this group the small, specialized schools like Juilliard, which offer an elite and affordable education to students with a particular outstanding talent in the performing arts.

Finally, there are a handful of unusual colleges, such as Cooper Union, that offer a great education at a low cost. Cooper Union was founded with the remit of training future artists and architects. Admission is highly competitive and based on artistic evaluation rather than conventional academic and extracurricular parameters.

For candidates with this very particular fit, this small group of institutions offers a wonderful alternative to mainstream education. Given their very particular academic orientation and the small numbers of students admitted, we will not discuss them at any length here, but if your particular fit leads you to this alternative group, the lessons offered in this book are still relevant.

More on Women's Colleges

Several women's colleges are featured on our Top 50 list of America's best colleges. Wellesley in particular has an impressive endowment, a highly respected faculty, and a student-teacher ratio of 8:1. With a 2017 admit rate of 28 percent (compared to single digits at coeducational, highly competitive colleges), Wellesley, along with other competitive women's colleges, presents an opportunity for a top-class education with less admissions pressure than an academically comparable coeducational college. Young, talented women inclined toward a women's college should certainly consider the alternative of applying to institutions like Wellesley and Smith College. These colleges would make particular sense for a Standard Strong woman without an additional hook.

Where Is Your Best Chance for Admission?

A funny thing happens when you compare the generally accepted Top 50 universities and Top 50 colleges with the 100 most selective universities and colleges, as reflected in admission rates. The lists don't *always* overlap. Does this mean that the top colleges and universities aren't really the most selective?

For the most part, the data is as we would expect: It matches well, with the top institutions also being the most selective. However, at the margins there are some exceptions of either special or unusual cases or some institutions that present a particular admissions opportunity. It's this latter category that is particularly interesting to many applicants.

The overall data on selective colleges includes those special and unusual institutions with very competitive admission rates. Cooper Union has the fifth lowest acceptance rate of all American colleges (lower than Yale), while the College of the Ozarks (which charges no tuition, asking students to work instead), has the eleventh lowest acceptance rate (lower than Brown).

Interestingly, only the forty-five *most* competitive institutions have admission rates below 20 percent. This presents a possible admissions opportunity. Your chances of getting into a high-quality institution with a rate of admission higher than that of the top forty-five institutions are a not-too-challenging 1 in 5. In 2012, twenty-five institutions had admission rates below 15 percent and only fourteen had admission rates in the single digits. For well-respected colleges like UVA, Colby, Oberlin, and Wellesley, the admission rate was approximately 1 in 3!

What are the top twenty-five institutions ranked in order of lowest admission rate? There are quite a few surprises. The following information is for the Class of 2016, compiled by *US News & World Report*.

The Most Difficult Colleges to Get Into in America

College	Overall Admit Rate
1. Harvard	6.1 percent
2. Stanford	6.6 percent
3. Curtis Institute of Music*	6.8 percent

4. United States Naval Academy*	6.8 percent
5. Cooper Union*	7.0 percent
6. Yale	7.1 percent
7. Juilliard School of Music*	7.35 percent
8. Columbia	7.4 percent
9. Princeton	7.9 percent
10. MIT	9.0 percent
11. United States Military Academy*	9.0 percent
12. College of the Ozarks*	9.5 percent
13. Brown	9.6 percent
14. Dartmouth	9.8 percent
15. United States Air Force Academy*	9.9 percent
16. Alice Lloyd College*	10.2 percent
17. Caltech	11.8 percent
18. United States Merchant Marine Academy*	12.4 percent
19. University of Pennsylvania (UPenn)	12.6 percent
20. Amherst	13.0 percent
21. Pomona	13.0 percent
22. University of Chicago	13.2 percent
23. Duke	13.4 percent
24. Claremont McKenna	13.6 percent
25. Swarthmore	14.2 percent

From this list of twenty-five institutions, more than a third (marked with an asterisk) can be classified as special and unusual institutions. Even MIT and Caltech serve a narrow, specialized sector of the applicant pool—those who are extremely gifted in science. If we re-rank with liberal arts institutions open to the general population of competitive college applicants, the list of the twenty-five most difficult colleges to get into looks quite different. Now you can dig deeper, all the way down to now twenty-fifth-ranked Washington University in St. Louis, which had a 17.9 percent acceptance rate in 2012. (For those of you who didn't do well on the math SAT, that means better than 1 in 6 applicants will be accepted, as opposed to Harvard's 1 in 16.)

Our revised list of the twenty-five most difficult mainstream colleges to get into in America now looks like this:

1. Harvard	6.1 percent
2. Stanford	6.6 percent
3. Yale	7.1 percent
4. Columbia	7.4 percent
5. Princeton	7.9 percent
6. Brown	9.6 percent
7. Dartmouth	9.8 percent
8. UPenn	12.6 percent
9. Amherst	13.0 percent
10. Pomona	13.0 percent
11. University of Chicago	13.2 percent
12. Duke	13.4 percent
13. Claremont	13.6 percent
14. Swarthmore	14.2 percent
15. Vanderbilt	14.2 percent
16. Northwestern	15.3 percent
17. Pitzer	15.7 percent
18. Bowdoin	15.8 percent

19. Cornell	16.6 percent
20. Rice	16.7 percent
21. Georgetown	17.0 percent
22. Williams	17.0 percent
23. Middlebury	17.2 percent
24. Johns Hopkins	17.7 percent
25. Washington University St. Louis	17.9 percent

Comparing College Rankings with Admission Rates

Let's take a closer look at the data to find additional quirks that may present unusual, favorable admissions opportunities. We're using the *US News & World Report* rankings not because we think it's a perfect ranking system but because, for lack of any better alternative, they have become a kind of proxy for ranking US institutions.

Things get interesting when we compare rankings for the best institutions with rankings of their admission rates. Theoretically, these should correlate fairly closely—and in general they do, particularly if we go through the exercise of removing the special and unusual institutions. As we would expect, the top ten colleges correspond with the top ten in terms of lowest admission rates. But if we dig a bit deeper, we start to see some truly eye-watering disparities between ranking and admission rates. For example, Duke is ranked the seventh best university, but it only has the twenty-second most difficult admission rate. There are a number of other prestigious institutions that similarly have *very large* gaps between their ranking and ease of being admitted.

These are *arbitrage* opportunities: colleges whose position in the rankings is fifteen or more positions higher than their position in the admission rate lists. These colleges have a negative arbitrage and present a favorable admissions opportunity. In other words, these are good colleges that are easier to get into than warranted by their relatively high position in the quality rankings. We have identified ten ranked institutions (out of the Top 50 universities and Top 50 colleges) as being particularly noteworthy, along with their Arbitrage Score (the difference between their ranking and their position on the admission rate list):

1. Duke and Cornell	15
2. University of Chicago	16
3. Tufts	21
4. University of Southern California	22
5. Washington University St. Louis	24
6. Johns Hopkins	25
7. Notre Dame	40
8. Emory	44
9. University of Virginia	55
10. College of William and Mary	66

Very few schools have positive arbitrage: a ranking that is *lower* than its admit rate. One of these is Brown, which is ranked fourteenth but is the twelfth hardest school to get into. In the case of Brown this makes sense considering the school's extremely positive image and claim to be among the very top schools in the country, given its relatively small size and limited graduate school offerings.

Financial Aid: How Much College Can You Afford?

Financial aid is a complicated and often confusing matter, one that this book doesn't deal with in great detail. With college fees sky-high and still rising, this is a crucial area for most students to research. With the exception of merit awards (such as academic or sports scholarships), financial aid is awarded on the basis of need, and only the very top colleges, which also happen to be the richest, have truly need-blind policies. Your access to several Top 50 colleges and universities will be, unfortunately, determined by your ability to pay the bills.

We have seen how nine of the twenty-five colleges with the lowest admission rates are special or unusual institutions with low costs of attendance. The very low acceptance rate at military academies, the College of the Ozarks, and even little Alice Lloyd College, which provides a free education to people from the Mountain States and has the sixteenth lowest acceptance rate in the country, reflects the overwhelming demand for less expensive (yet still competitive) educational opportunities. And in some sense, the very high academic rankings of Harvard, Yale, Princeton, and other top colleges that follow a need-blind admissions policy also reflect the financial inequality of American society. If they didn't provide entry to students on a need-blind basis, would they continue to receive more than 30,000 applications every year? And would admission rates therefore continue to hover around 6 percent? Likely not.

Be aware of differences in terminology and policy across colleges. "Need-blind" is very different from "need-sensitive" or "need-aware." Only a small subset of top colleges is truly need-blind, with admissions decisions *completely* independent of a student's financial circumstances. Once admitted, however, there are differences in the amount of financial aid available. Only the richest colleges can hold to the promise of meeting an admitted student's full financial-aid need.

Unless a college has a clear need-blind admissions policy, they may well favor fee-paying candidates over students requiring financial assistance. College is a business, after all—even if a not-for-profit one! Need-sensitive or need-aware colleges do take into account a student's ability to pay when making admissions decisions and, consequently, reserve a section of the admissions slots for full-paying students.

US Institutions that are need-blind for US and international students

Amherst
Dartmouth
Harvard
MIT
Princeton
Yale

US Institutions that are need-blind for US students only

Barnard

Boston College

Bowdoin

Brandeis

Caltech

Claremont

Holy Cross

Columbia

Davidson

Emory

Georgetown

Grinnell

Hamilton

Haverford

Harvey Mudd

Johns Hopkins

Middlebury

Northwestern

UPenn

Pomona

Rice

Stanford

Swarthmore

University of Chicago

University of Miami

University of Michigan

University of North Carolina, Chapel Hill
Notre Dame
University of Richmond
University of Rochester
University of Southern California
University of Virginia
Vanderbilt
Vassar
Wellesley
Williams

Note that many colleges that are need-blind for all US applicants are not need-blind for US transfer students or for foreign students. I regularly suggest to my own clients that when applying to the most competitive colleges, you cannot let financial aid be a factor in deciding where to apply. Almost all of the very top colleges can meet all (or almost all) of your genuinely demonstrated need. In the very rare case where there is a gap, it's likely worth managing the shortfall from personal resources because, as you now know from our discussion on branding, investing in top colleges will likely enhance your future earning power.

Playing the Early Application Card

EARLY VS. REGULAR APPLICATIONS

The decision to apply early is important for both students and colleges.

For students, playing "the early card" sends a clear signal of "top choice" to your dream college. This signal is most powerful where early decisions are binding or restrictive. For all students applying early and who have judged their competitive fit correctly, there is the possibility of early success and of avoiding months of extra regular application work and stress. Early applicants are usually a self-selecting group of highly competitive students and early acceptance rates reflect this. For the Class of 2017 applying to the Ivy League, the average early acceptance rate was 21.6 percent compared with a regular acceptance rate of 7.5 percent. We have compared the data for early and regular acceptance rates for the Class of 2007 and 2017. What is clear is that the acceptance rate for early applicants is now far greater—almost three times as high—lending credence to the view that early applicants are a select pool of highly competitive students comprising a number of student athletes and other SuperCombos.

Colleges also play the early vs. regular acceptance game and are keen to access this group of highly competitive candidates. At the most competitive colleges, almost half the class is filled by early applications. For Harvard's Class of 2018, a full 49 percent of the class was admitted through their early action program. You can clearly see that for the most competitive candidates, there is an advantage to playing the early card.

Early acceptances, particularly binding decisions, have the effect of locking in acceptances and consequently pushing up college yield. And colleges are acutely aware of the prestige associated with high yield numbers.

A WORD ABOUT YIELD

Yield is the percentage of admitted students who accept their offer of admission and enroll in a particular institution. It's an important number in understanding the college admissions process. Colleges with the highest yields tend to be the most difficult to get into, because most students who are admitted truly want to go to that college. For instance, looking at yield for 2017, Harvard has the highest yield at 82 percent. The difference between Harvard's high yield and 100 percent comes from the small number of applicants who will be admitted to multiple top colleges in any given year—SuperCombos who are equally in demand at all the top colleges. These students may have particular reasons, such as generous financial-aid offers, for picking one top college over another. And remember, choice within a group—even the top group of colleges—is not particularly determinative of future success.

Colleges compete with each other on yield because it is, quite simply, a prestige issue with direct benefits for college rankings and fundraising activities.

Let's look at college yield figures for the Class of 2017. It's by no means a comprehensive list but will give a sense of yield at most of the top (and some less competitive) colleges.

Class of 2017: Yield

Top Colleges

Harvard	82 percent
Stanford	77 percent
Yale	72 percent
Princeton	67 percent
UPenn	64 percent
Brown	59 percent

University of Chicago	54 percent
Claremont	53 percent
Cornell	53 percent
Dartmouth	48 percent
Other Colleges	
Middlebury	42 percent
University of Michigan	41 percent
Bates	40 percent
Johns Hopkins	38 percent
William & Mary	31 percent
Emory	29 percent
Dickinson	25 percent
Boston University	21 percent

EARLY APPLICATIONS: THE TWO WAYS TO APPLY EARLY

1. Binding Early *Decision:* Students can apply to only one college early and must accept their offer if they are admitted.
2. Nonbinding Early *Action:* If admitted, students do not have to accept their offer of admission.

2a. *Restrictive Early Action:* Allows a student to apply early to one college only. Single-choice early application is a variation on the restrictive option, offered by Yale and Princeton, where students can also apply early action *only* to state universities or colleges offering rolling admissions, in addition to their Yale or Princeton applications.

Early Decision Flow Chart

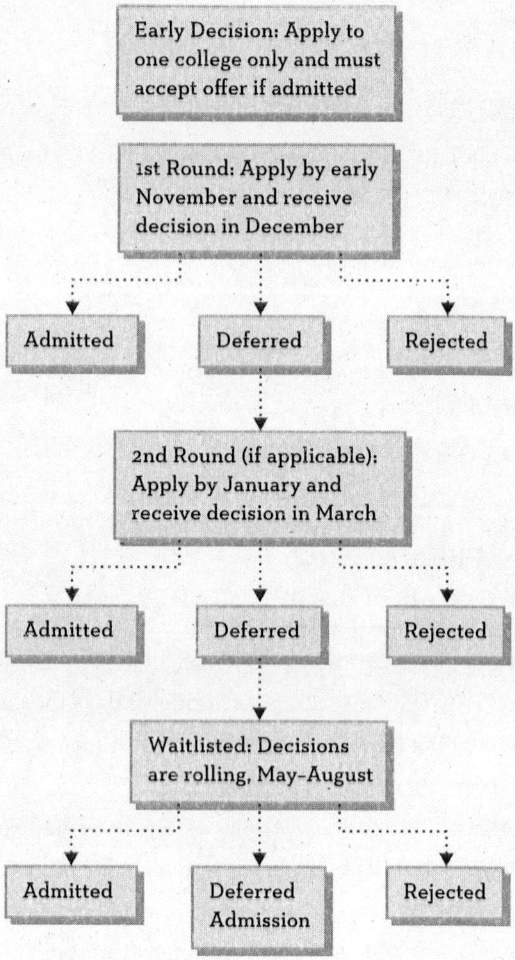

Early Action Flow Chart

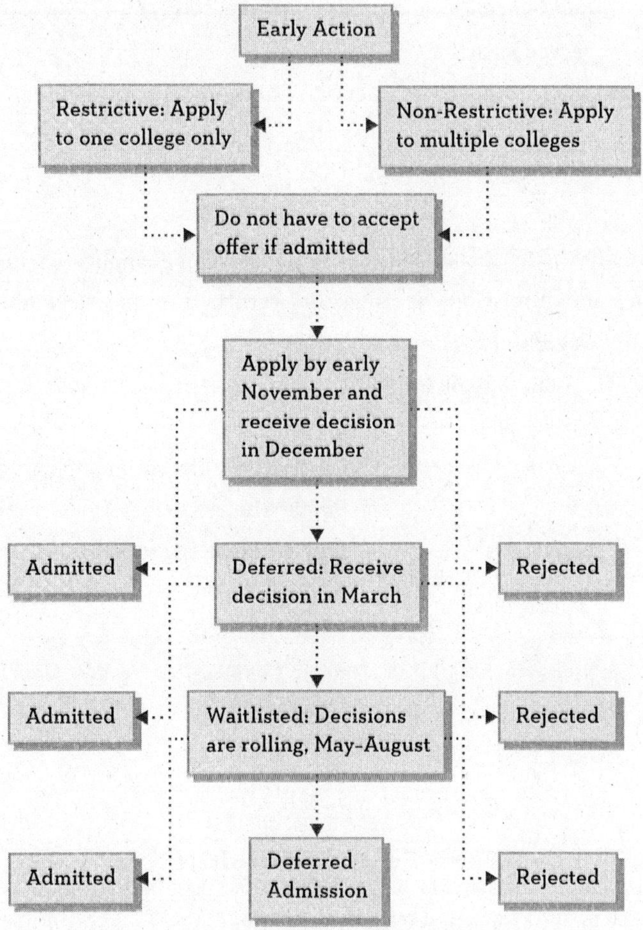

Rolling admissions programs have flexible application windows and do not subscribe to conventional application dates; instead, candidates are evaluated on a first-come, first-served basis.

2b. *Nonrestrictive Early Action:* Allows students to apply early to multiple colleges (other than colleges that have restrictive admissions policies).

Most early applications have early November application deadlines and admissions decisions are returned in mid-December—before regular applications are due.

The Ivies use the following early admissions systems:

Harvard	Restrictive Early Action
Yale	Single Choice Early Action
Princeton	Single Choice Early Action
Columbia	Early Decision
Brown	Early Decision
UPenn	Early Decision
Dartmouth	Early Decision
Cornell	Early Decision

SECOND-ROUND EARLY DECISIONS

Occasionally, some of the less competitive colleges—e.g., Wesleyan, Tufts, Emory—offer a second round (or second chance) at early decisions, with applications accepted in January. The rationale is to encourage continued commitment from an earlier, unsuccessful applicant or to capture talent that has been unsuccessful with an early application at a more competitive institution.

Early applicants would hope to be admitted or deferred. If you are rejected, you likely misjudged your competitive strength. If you are deferred, you will have to very quickly get to work strengthening your deferred application while also filing all your regular applications. This will require introspection and thoughtful consideration as to where you can strengthen or work your hook to boost your competitive strength. You will also need to carefully and productively manage the limited time between early decision outcomes and regular application due dates. (We'll discuss the "get back to work" strategy in greater detail in our discussion on waitlists.)

Ivy League Early vs. Regular Admissions Statistics

CLASS OF 2007			
College	Regular Acceptance Rate (Percent)	Early Acceptance Rate (Percent)	Percent of Class Filled by Early Applications
Brown	13.3	25.8	N/A
Columbia	9.6	31.7	43
Cornell	29.4	40.7	37
Dartmouth	16	32.4	37

College	Regular Acceptance Rate (Percent)	Early Acceptance Rate (Percent)	Percent of Class Filled by Early Applications
Harvard	6.8	15.1	N/A
UPenn	17.2	38.9	47
Princeton	7.3	25.1	49.5
Yale	9.6	21.3	43

CLASS OF 2017

College	Regular Acceptance Rate (percent)	Early Acceptance Rate (percent)	Percent of Class Filled by Early Applications
Brown	8.1	18.5	36.8
Columbia	5.6	19.2	43.2
Cornell	13.5	29.5	38.9
Darmouth	8.6	29.4	41.4
Harvard	3.8	18.4	N/A
UPenn	9.8	24.9	49.4
Princeton	5.4	18.3	N/A
Yale	5.3	14.4	N/A

If you are a competitive fit—preferably a SuperCombo, but certainly a Combo—we advise applying early. While there may be some disadvantage to applying early (particularly for students in need of financial aid where binding early decisions could limit admissions offers) the pluses outweigh the minuses. For highly competitive students, you have clearly identified and signaled your top choice and have the possibility of early success. If you need to evaluate the best possible financial aid package on offer, consider an early application over an early decision. In general, playing the early card is a good idea for the strongest applicants.

Regular Applications

Earlier in this chapter, I sounded a note of caution on diminishing returns from applying to too many colleges. More is not better. A selection of between eight to ten colleges can cover the safe, balanced range needed to ensure a rational and successful application strategy. If you have correctly judged your competitive fit, you should not need more than ten options to succeed.

Dream colleges: 2–3
Solid colleges: 3–4
Safety colleges: 2–3

Admissions decisions (usually made by the end of March) bring three possibilities: admit, reject, waitlist.

Not unlike the deferred outcome we discussed in the context of early applications, waitlists require extra work from the candidate. For a waitlisted student, the goal is to be proactive, attempting to climb to the top of the waitlist basket.

So how does one do that? Stay in regular touch with the admissions office, updating them on recent validations, awards, and accomplishments. Strengthen your fit by gaining additional, *meaningful* credentials within a short time period. If you cannot garner these from your existing hooks, create new ones. If you can work the legacy hook, do so now!

Make sure your school communicates directly with admissions officers to support your efforts. Ask teachers and counselors to write additional letters on recent outstanding academic and extracurricular accomplishments. Reinforce your commitment to your dream college and assure the admissions office that their college remains your top choice and that, if admitted, you will attend. This is your last shot to play the admissions game, so give it all you've got. Someone is getting off that waitlist and into the freshman class—make sure you have done everything legitimately possible to make sure it's you.

Simply put, the right college *is* where you best fit. And when your fit is right you have a good chance, once admitted, of success—both in the admissions process and in college life and beyond.

Learn about the colleges in the different groups and use opportunities such as Admissions Arbitrage, early admissions, and financial aid to your advantage. And continue to focus on the underlying theme that living life holistically, being the best you can be, will lead you to the right college with greater ease and success.

CHAPTER FOURTEEN

Crafting the Perfect Application

You have found your fit, worked your hooks to become a *competitive* fit, and made a list of your preferred colleges. So how do we now put together an application that offers the best chance of attending one of those colleges? This chapter explains how to mix all those ingredients together and create your best application basket in a manner that communicates your best self.

I focus on a holistic process, taking into account the whole person and all aspects of life. If you have prepared yourself well for life, chances are you have prepared yourself well to be a successful college applicant. The holistic life approach benefits the college process as it flows from the initial through to the final stage.

Personal Growth → Fit → Competitive Fit →
Right College → Best Application

Preparing or constructing your application basket is your final opportunity to present your best self. And this is a part of the process almost entirely within your control (I say *almost* because you'll obviously have limited control over letters of recommendation).

It is important to remember that the admissions process is not an exact science and there remains an element of intuition guiding an admissions officer's decision making. Often, it is the intangibles that tip the balance. Indeed, how you present yourself in areas such as the application essay can help tip the balance in your favor.

Think of creating your best application in the same way as assembling a desirable basket. You control what goes into this basket and each ingredient contributes to its desirability. Your basket's overall value is assessed as the weighted value of its individual ingredients, though there is no magic number or specific value attached to any one ingredient. We are focusing on America's top colleges, so your AI must be solid. Mediocre grades and SAT scores below the 700 mark simply won't cut it for the most competitive colleges unless, of course, there is another truly significant hook that lifts the weighted value of your ingredients.

The value of your competitive fit can further benefit from "showcasing"—the presenting of your achievements in the most favorable way. There is an important element of selling yourself in the admissions process. Whether it is through your essay or interview, learn how to present yourself in the best possible way. This is where students are advised to sell themselves, to sound humble while bragging.

Application Basket—the Key Ingredients

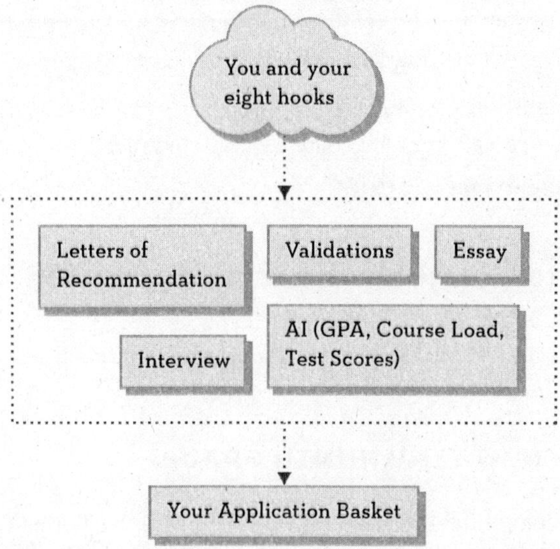

Correctly done, showcasing can complement your ingredients and make your application basket look like a must-have. This works best when the underlying ingredients are strong and genuine. It's most certainly not about concocting ingredients, nor is it about flooding the admissions office with superfluous material: Additional letters from employers, alumni, major donors, or celebrities are only useful to communicate an additional hook not reflected elsewhere in your application package.

For Standard Strong candidates with good but not great ingredients, a great presentation becomes more important to supplement your Standard Strong application. A great essay, letter of recommendation, or personal interview could make the difference between deferred, waitlisted, and admitted.

Seen from an admissions officer's perspective, your application basket is a window through which to observe you in your own habitat, getting a sense of the real you. Have you appropriately window-dressed your ingredients and convinced the reader of your unique competitive fit?

How to Create the Perfect Application

Work hard! Plan well! And follow this application timeline!

FRESHMAN YEAR (NINTH GRADE)

Establish a solid foundation for leadership via the Three A's. Join organizations you could later lead.

SOPHOMORE YEAR (TENTH GRADE)

Take any SAT II's related to a course you are taking in your current curriculum. If you take physics in tenth grade, for example, take the physics SAT II at the *end* of your sophomore year.

Foreign students need to pay particular attention to the content of specific SAT II subject tests as they match closely the US taught curriculum. And be aware that science test content can be quite different from similar classes in the UK and Europe.

Start detailed application planning and preparing for standardized tests. Determine whether you need outside test preparation help. If you opt for SAT tutoring, plan to take the SAT I test soon after the tutoring course. Fall of junior year is a good time to take the SAT I.

Solidify your involvement and move up in organizations you have joined.

JUNIOR YEAR (ELEVENTH GRADE)

September–October: Take the SAT I

It's not recommended to take the SAT I prior to junior year. Remember the danger of burnout and application fatigue. Many competitive applicants get particularly stressed about standardized testing and start taking them as early as their freshman year in high school. This is a mistake. If you are going to perform well on them in ninth grade, you'll do even better by eleventh grade. If you are thinking of the early test attempt as practice, you're better off practicing at home. Don't waste your energy and (your parents') financial resources.

Take a leadership position in your chosen organizations and activities.

December

Take multiple SAT II's (two if you haven't taken any or if you are unsatisfied with your score from an earlier test).

January

Additional date for SAT I or SAT II, retakes, or additional subject tests.

May

Additional opportunity to take SAT I or SAT II. Start identifying teachers to write your letters of recommendation.

July

Think about essay topics. Essay topics vary little from year to year; if the current Common Application is not yet online, use last year's as a guide. Think of which teachers might write your best letters of recommendation.

August

Start writing college applications.

SENIOR YEAR (TWELFTH GRADE):

September

Lock in your letters of recommendation and finalize early application choices.

October

Yet another chance to take SAT I or SAT II.

November

Early application deadlines. *Last chance* for SAT I or II for early application.

December

Early admission decisions: If you are admitted, you may have completed your journey. If not, you must now follow the regular application timeline. And it's time to work additional hooks if you are deferred.

Regular application deadlines in mid- to late December.

Yet another chance for SAT I or SAT II.

January

Last chance to take SAT I or II for use on regular application.

March

Regular admission decisions. Evaluate your offers. If you have multiple, competitive offers move into decision-making mode. This may be the time to arrange college visits to weigh competing offers. Time to work additional hooks if you are waitlisted.

May

Time to make your decision and accept your best offer.

Mobilize Your Team

Consider the players—family, friends, and educators—who can add value to your application process. "The outside world never lies," so make sure you've been objective in assessing your own competitive strengths. How you present your fit must be in sync with how others perceive you.

FAMILY

You (and your application) will benefit from family support. Their support is both emotionally and practically important. Apart from the nurture factor, there is the matter of soaring education costs and your decision might be contingent upon your parents' ability and desire to financially subsidize it. Share information, ideas, and strategy with your family. Make sure you are on the same page.

Friends and family friends—particularly those familiar with the college environment—are a useful extension of your team and can be valuable sounding boards, providing much needed reality checks.

EDUCATORS

Teachers and school counselors can be helpful guides and mentors, providing independent validations. Educators are also responsible for an important piece of the application: the letters of recommendation. Most colleges require two teacher recommendations and an additional report from a school counselor. Admissions officers place great value on their colleagues' views and consider them to be objective voices in your application. Make sure you have built a positive relationship with your counselor and teachers and that they mirror your views of your appropriate fit. Your recommenders need to go beyond describing you as Standard Strong and advertise you as an outstanding, unique student. Be mindful of your timeline, allowing plenty of time for them to write their letters. Remember, you aren't the only student applying to college! With less time pressure, your teachers are likely to write more considered—and more effective—letters.

The significance of genuine, superlative-filled recommendations is particularly relevant for international students. American teachers tend to have less difficulty selling a favored student, a trait that other (perhaps more reserved) cultures have trouble matching. If you are a foreign student, educate your teachers on the showcasing aspect of the process. Recommendations also provide a good opportunity for foreign teachers to clarify basic differences in areas such as grading, ranking, length of the school day, and extracurricular offerings. Many foreign high schools—notably in Europe and parts of Asia—simply don't offer the array of extracurricular and enrichment opportunities increasingly associated with American schools and required by top-tier American universities.

Liberal arts colleges appreciate versatile students and it's advisable to select recommenders from a diverse range of subjects.

If your teachers believe in your competitive fit, there's every chance you'll be recommended as a must-have college student. With a shared belief in your fit, your teachers and counselors are more likely to remain engaged with your application as it passes through stages that might include deferrals and waitlists.

Counselors at top schools often have strong links and access to admissions officers at top colleges. And support from your school is particularly important if there's a tradition of several students applying to top colleges (this is often the case for students at elite private high schools). Members of your school's faculty are then more likely to have clout and credibility with admissions officers and perhaps even college faculty.

A positive, credible relationship with your school will also insulate you from unpleasant surprises. Several elite schools monitor and stipulate where students may apply, in effect hijacking your ability to define the right college for you. Remember, educators have a responsibility to the overall student body and the institution they serve. If you are a part of an overall placement strategy, that may not serve your individual interests. So be realistic about defining your competitive fit and be proactive about nurturing relationships with your school's staff. It's within your control to ensure that your best interests are served.

You Need Cheerleaders

WORK EXPERIENCE

Plan your high school summers! Interesting summers create worthwhile experiences. While generally good for your growth and maturity in life, such experiences can also be useful for your college application. For instance, a summer job can add depth and credibility to your particular interests or hooks. If student government is your niche, go to Washington and work for your senator. Interested in regenerative medicine? Find a summer internship alongside scientists conducting stem cell research! These experiences can also provide valuable contacts. Your employer could very well be connected to your dream college as an alumnus, professionally, or both. Reflections on significant summer experiences are often the basis for engaging application essays, and summer work experiences can be the source for unique letters of recommendation.

OUTSIDE PROFESSIONALS

As competition—and parental budgets—have increased, so too has the demand for test preparation companies, tutors, and admissions consultants. Whether this increased demand is results-driven, peer pressure–driven, or simply based on need, the college-readiness industry is growing at a rapid clip. Outside professionals can provide useful, objective, focused help. However, tutors and consultants are not a substitute for a student's own hard work.

CASE STUDY: Nazneen: Iranian American from Los Angeles

Type: White—California—US Citizen—Upper Income

Like many Americans of Middle Eastern heritage, Iranians

often fall through the race cracks, failing to benefit from this hook.

Background: Naz was a talented, focused American high school student with dreams of attending an Ivy League college. On paper, she looked very much like a Standard Strong candidate: top grades at her competitive private school; strong test scores; a range of recognizable, impressive activities (school newspaper editor, student government vice president, strong involvement in drama). She was well regarded by her peers and teachers and generally considered among the high achievers at her competitive school.

Challenge: How to use Naz's background and solid credentials to push her from Standard Strong to "uniquely interesting" by making use of a particular hook.

Plan of Action: Fortunately, Naz began thinking about her college application process early. Her personal journey had recently taken her to Iran, the country of her roots. Traveling across Tehran, she realized she had a life beyond the palm-fringed boulevards of distant Los Angeles. Her ninth grade classroom suddenly seemed very far away. Naz's cultural awakening would benefit her personal growth and maturity and, in turn, her college application.

Returning to Iran for her subsequent summer breaks, she perfected her Farsi and arranged to work at a Tehran-based women's rights foundation. She began redefining her own identity, as an Iranian living in America rather than as an Iranian American. By the end of high school, Naz had gone from halting to fluent Farsi, had identified with a "politically correct" women's movement in an Islamic country, and had taken the women's rights foundation in a new direction by setting up a vocational school for young women in Bam, a region ravaged by powerful earthquakes. She even managed to integrate her two worlds by organizing a Los Angeles fundraiser to purchase computer equipment for the school in Bam.

Solution: By focusing on the unique, Naz was able to create a strong extracurricular hook: Iranian American women's rights activist. She became a community leader. She was no longer another Standard Strong Iranian American applicant from Los Angeles. She was now a dynamic Iranian woman and community leader—one who happened to live in Los Angeles. She was now Nazneen when navigating the streets of Tehran and Naz in her native Los Angeles.

Practical, Positive Advantage: Naz was able to translate her successful personal journey into a successful college application. Her college essay chronicled her unique experience in Bam and how it shaped her goals. She detailed her belief that women's empowerment is the backbone of wider social change, particularly in Islamic countries. A discourse on women's empowerment in earthquake-ravaged Bam was a unique essay among American college applicants.

Her work, commitment, and emerging leadership skills didn't go unnoticed by her peers and teachers. What would have been Standard Strong letters of recommendation now packed an added punch of community leader, feminist, and peer role model.

Result: Naz was able to push her fit from Standard Strong to a competitive Combo—combining Standard Strong student with an outstanding talent, community leader. Naz received an early action offer from an Ivy League college. She also received two regular-decision Ivy League acceptances.

CHAPTER FIFTEEN

Writing the Perfect Essay

College essays are often the best way to make sure your own voice will be heard. It's your unique opportunity to help the admissions office know your best self and to sell yourself as a must-have in the incoming freshman class. Essays also provide admissions officers with a powerful tool to assess your competitive fit. To capitalize on this opportunity, your essay must convey a unique voice with an original, imaginative, and well-written story. Remember that competitive colleges receive thousands of applications. Admissions officers at the nation's most competitive colleges read upwards of 30,000 essays every year. It is imperative to write a standout rather than standard form essay.

- Start early. Time management is important. Essay topics vary little from year to year. Summer before senior year is a good time to start planning your essay. Applications are usually online by early August.

- Tell an interesting, imaginative story. *Do not write a report.* Structure your essay correctly, arriving at a logical, powerful, and meaningful conclusion. Focus on your story's arc, but style and structure are equally important.
- Your essay should always have a positive, upbeat message. Sound an optimistic note!
- Don't be scared to humblebrag (which is exactly what it sounds like: sounding humble while actually bragging). You are, after all, selling yourself.
- Go for emotional impact: coming-out story, sob story, save-the-world story, unusual story. Use the essay to subtly reinforce your unique fit. Remember, your essay is part of your overall application, so be consistent. Continue to focus on your competitive hooks. Think of your powerful, unique story and then back into an essay topic that will accommodate what you want to say.
- Humor is an important tool. Used correctly, with maturity and sensitivity, humor has universal appeal and can enhance your essay with a light, appealing touch. Remember, your reader is wading through several thousand essays. Comic relief can benefit your application. But use it also to reflect your wisdom and maturity, because funny is appealing only when used appropriately!
- Tailor your essay to what you know about a particular college. Be guided also by the admissions officer's perspective: Do you fit what they are looking for to fill the freshman class? Show that you have done your research and found that you are an ideal fit for your dream college.

- Stay with what is politically correct. While a skillfully crafted sob story is beneficial to revealing your unique fit, essays that clearly reflect or even hint at socioeconomic advantage or connections are not. Do not write about the opulent summer experience that your parents arranged and paid for.
- "Optional" essays are, in fact, must-do essays. You are applying to America's most competitive colleges. As mentioned, this area can make the difference between Standard Strong and well-qualified candidates. You have to compete fully—*nothing* is optional!

Real Examples from the Common Application

Almost all top colleges use the Common Application to aggregate individual application requirements.

The 2014 Common Application offered a choice of five essay questions. If you carefully parse these five questions you can see how the same general theme can be employed to answer any of them—the questions aren't deeply differentiated. It's all about focusing on the story you want to write and how you write it. Think creatively. Start with the best essay you want to write. Get your essay ready, regardless of the questions, and then see which of the five questions it can most readily be adapted to answer.

There is simply no way that your best essay cannot be adapted to fit one of the five broad questions from the Common Application. Don't let the actual wording of the questions throw you off. These are indistinct, open-ended, general questions, and inevitably can be summed up as "tell us something uniquely interesting about you."

THE 2014 COMMON APPLICATION ESSAY QUESTIONS

1. "Some students have a background or story that is so central to their identity that they believe their application would be incomplete without it. If this sounds like you, then please share your story."

At first glance, this question is a not-so-subtle invitation to discuss your racial, ethnic, or socioeconomic background, without explicitly saying so. If you are from *any* minority group or have overcome *any* disadvantage, this question is for you. It is also tailor-made for foreign students who should seize this opportunity to highlight their distinct cultural niche. However, this question is open to interpretation and might also be answered by a wealthy, white student who has done something interesting and off-script. It can be successfully answered by anyone and, as you will notice in subsequent questions, the same answer can be used for all five potential essay topics.

So if you have a relevant, politically correct central story to tell—if you are a minority, foreign student, or have a socioeconomic hook—this question is a perfect choice. Construct your essay to showcase your competitive fit: How did your central story affect you? What did you learn from this seminal experience and how did it contribute to your maturity?

A "maturity story" should focus on your personal growth and wisdom. While intelligence is easily manifested in the data component of your application, it's often difficult to convey this aspect of your personality. Apart from the interview, your essay is the only area where your maturity and emotional intelligence can be expressed.

Your story should end positively, with a wiser, enhanced "you." Write a powerful conclusion reflecting upon learned lessons and personal growth. If you committed yourself to community activism, perhaps you learned the importance of compromise, tempering unbridled idealism with a dose of realism. It was this on-the-ground experience that helped you achieve a more practical, mature, and workable solution to your community's problems.

It's important to use your hooks and personal journey of growth to maximum advantage. Whether or not your story has a happy ending, you're still sounding a positive note by confronting the lessons learned along the way. Apart from wanting the best academic candidates, colleges also want socially well-adjusted candidates. Colleges know that high school stars are plentiful in a competitive freshman college class. How will you make that transition from *the* star to one among many stars? Are you that community activist who succeeded in trading a comfort zone for an adventure through the unknown? Your essay is a valuable opportunity to tell such stories and showcase your hooks, intelligence, and maturity.

2. "Recount an incident or time when you experienced failure. How did it affect you, and what lessons did you learn?"

You don't have to think hard to determine that the time you experienced failure might be exactly the same as the story that is central to your identity in question one.

There are two basic approaches to answer this type of question:

Humblebragging—Describe a failure that really isn't much of a failure. For example, tell the story of how you came in second in a national poetry contest—a failure because you didn't come in first. The athletics version of the humblebrag? "Our team lost in the national championships."

Humblebragging can show that there is much to learn from the "failure" of coming in second: how to be humble in the face of a better opponent; the need for more practice, commitment, and resolve; and the joys of pushing yourself to be the best you can be.

Do *not* use this approach if you failed by a large margin. If you came in last place or if your team didn't make it out of its bracket in a national tournament, it starts to sound more like you actually *did* fail. It's important to write about almost winning and failing in achieving your goal of being the best. While "everyone isn't a winner" in college admissions, humblebragging can subtly show you to be a winner by losing!

The Life Lesson—Write an essay about when you actually *did* experience failure, but learned an important lesson that pushed you to achieve a major success (possibly in another pursuit). In college essays, a failure *must* be leavened with a subsequent success. Just learning lessons in an abstract manner isn't the point of the college essay. You need to push further, actually applying the lessons learned. Your story needs to be either redemptive or reflect an achievement borne out of a failure and never feel like a downer.

An example could be that you failed to get the lead in a school play. From this failure, you learned that you needed to be more in touch with your feelings, better communicating them through your acting. This experience forged a more open, mature person. Your new awareness, sensitivity, and emotional sophistication led you to explore drama as a means of helping special-needs students express themselves, an activity you ultimately found more personally rewarding than appearing as the lead in a school play. Indeed, you are now thinking of becoming a child psychologist and are applying to Dartmouth on the stellar reputation of its undergraduate psychology department.

3. "Reflect on a time when you challenged a belief or idea. What prompted you to act? Would you make the same decision again?"

Could it be that the time you challenged a belief or idea was the time you "experienced failure"? It most certainly could have been if things didn't go as planned. If they did, that plucky challenge might be the same story that is so "central to your identity" in question 1.

4. "Describe a place or environment where you are perfectly content. What do you experience there, and why is it meaningful to you?"

That special place might be the place where you experienced failure or where a story that is central to your identity occurred. Or maybe it's a place where you challenged a belief or idea.

5. "Discuss an accomplishment or event, formal or informal, that marked your transition from childhood to adulthood within your culture, community, or family."

This question is also aimed squarely at disadvantaged or minority students who might not have the same record of validations (awards, medals, victories in competitions, high grades, etc.) as a wealthy, white student. The giveaway is the phrase *within your culture:* The admissions officers are most definitely not expecting an essay that begins with, "In the white, Anglo-Saxon, Protestant culture of Greenwich, Connecticut, getting your first car is a very important event." For admissions purposes, white students from Greenwich will typically not have the option of playing the culture card, whereas Hispanics, African Americans, Native Americans, and Asian Americans can. White students are not similarly culturally interesting, unless they are recent immigrants or have preserved their culture (a Bosnian American child of refugees would be an example of a culturally interesting white applicant).

A privileged, white student might have a community (and certainly has a family), but unless there is something compelling about your transition from childhood to adulthood, I would recommend staying away from this essay topic. As mentioned earlier, it's generally not to your advantage to tell a story of privilege. But it might be that your transition from childhood to adulthood involved one of the following:

- A story that is central to your identity
- A time you experienced failure
- A time you challenged a belief or idea
- A place or environment where you were perfectly content

It isn't hard to see that these essay topics are sufficiently broad and that any prepared answer can be readily adapted to fit any of the questions. If you begin by trying to tailor your answer to a specific question, you might miss out on a compelling essay topic.

CHAPTER SIXTEEN

Nailing the College Interview

Interviews give you the opportunity to meet and interact with a representative from your dream college. While not all colleges offer interviews—and those that do generally rely on alumni interviewers—if you have the option of an interview, take it. Remember, for competitive college admissions, anything listed as optional is actually a must-do.

There is no science to the amount of weight these interviews add to your application basket. Interviews can be tie-breakers between two qualified candidates, an opportunity to fact-check the applicant, or even a public relations effort (only the wealthiest colleges have an alumni network able to cover personal interviews, something that keeps alumni engaged and could encourage students to apply). The exact function of the interview can differ widely, but what is important to remember is that a bad interview can harm your chances! It is entirely possible that your interview is assigned to an important alumnus. Turn to your mantra (and your charm) and see the interview as a valuable opportunity to showcase your competitive fit. Be the best you can be. Reinforce your belief that you belong at that college!

The Dirty Little Secrets to a Great Interview

- Bring a copy of your résumé to the interview. A résumé provides a clear, unambiguous record of your background and achievements and helps set the stage for the interview. Some listed achievement, interest, or extracurricular activity will likely provoke the interviewer's first question, preventing the possibility of a vague and unspecific opener ("Tell me something about yourself").

  A résumé also establishes confidence in your candidacy. Make sure all your academic information is on your résumé. When asked for scores or grades, slippery answers like "I don't recall" leave the impression of a poor candidate likely shielding a poor academic record. You will be surprised at just how useful a résumé can be in establishing a comfortable conversation. A relaxed atmosphere helps you take charge by steering discussion to areas on your résumé reflective of your competitive fit.
- It might seem blindingly obvious, but it deserves repeating: Be early. And even more obvious, but also worth stressing: Don't even *think* of arriving late.
- While there is no formal dress code, don't be sloppy. Avoid jeans. In case you were wondering, yoga or gym clothes are a definite no.

  You do not have to change your personality. Thankfully,

everyone is not an extrovert. So whether you're introverted or extroverted, you still need to display self-confidence. Look your interviewer in the eye, speak clearly, and avoid larding your sentences with *umm* and *like*.

- Be friendly but not overly familiar. Certain topics—personal life, religion, and politics—are no-go areas, and your interviewer has likely been instructed to avoid these subjects. But if your résumé reflects a strong political interest or engagement in social issues, then bring it up in a straightforward, nonconfrontational way. This is also true for religion. If you went to a religious school or were involved in a faith-based charity or activity, this too can be a worthy topic of conversation. Evaluate your interviewer when discussing sensitive or controversial matters. If you are being interviewed by someone who is much older or who clearly is a social conservative and you are agitating for a Marxist revolution, don't discard your principles but try to take a more dispassionate, academic approach. By all means have a vibrant—even passionate—discussion, but never, ever antagonize your interviewer.
- Be respectful, but don't be fearful of taking charge. Don't always wait for the interviewer to ask you questions. As with essay topics, nudge the conversation into areas that highlight your particular fit. For instance, if there is a lull in the conversation, jump in before an uncomfortable silence settles in. Offer an opinion on a newsworthy topic related to your particular academic or extracurricular interest. You can keep the interview flowing while also highlighting another aspect of your personality and interests.

- Make it known that you are interviewing for your dream college. It never hurts to clearly reaffirm that the interviewer is questioning you on behalf of your top choice. Make sure you have done enough research about the target college to be enthusiastic about its institutional strengths, especially those relating to your fit. Say you, the editor of your high school literary magazine, were at a Yale interview. Be prepared to note specific professors in Yale's first-class English department (and even examples of their work), while stressing your excitement at possibly learning from Yale luminaries whose work provided helpful insight when you were editing your school's literary magazine.
- Do your homework! Try to find out something about your interviewer and identify areas of common interest. Ask about his or her college experience.
- Research the college and discuss why you believe it's the right college for you. Come prepared with topical, original questions about the college. In today's online world this is easily done; start by reading the college newspaper online. You might be surprised to find that many alumni interviewers are very familiar with current issues at their alma mater.
- Prepare yourself for the very common but nevertheless very tricky interview question: "What unique attributes make you a more desirable candidate than the many others applying to our college?" Establish that you hold yourself to extremely high standards. Confident students tend to set their own bar rather than reach for one set by others. Make it clear that you're

that type of student, striving to be the best you can be. Do not compare yourself to other candidates.

- Talk about a specific incident that highlights how you successfully handled a challenging situation. Telling your story should also emphasize your competitive fit. Let's say that you're the editor of your school newspaper and in following complaints from female students against a particular teacher you make the risky decision to run a story on the controversy. Indeed, controversial topics are usually a forbidden zone for school newspaper editors, but you make a tough editorial decision and, under your leadership, that trend is reversed. As you follow the story, several classmates come forward to share their experiences, concerns, and fears, and you win the support of your peers, which catapults you into a leadership role.

  Recounting this story, you have highlighted the following attributes: moral courage, original thinking, problem solving, and initiative. You have demonstrated that you're a leader among your peers worthy of admission to your dream college. And your interviewer will likely identify you as an "outstanding personality" and make the case that you should be admitted over other Standard Strong candidates.
- It's a good idea to discuss your nonacademic interests. Admissions interviewers too use a holistic approach.
- It never hurts to write a thank-you note.

"Congratulations, You've Been Accepted!"

There is nothing more gratifying, more inspiring, than tearing open that envelope from your dream college to find that your hard work, determination, and strategic planning have paid off—you've been accepted to one of America's most selective universities.

As you have now seen, the college admissions process doesn't have to be a stressful, high-stakes game. There is a method for getting into a top college with relative calm. And it's important to remember that *you* are in control of the process, *not* the other way around. The path to admission must evolve holistically, as part of a life directed by a mantra of being your best self, by setting clear, consistent, and realistic goals. Students nurtured with such a mantra will mature with discipline and focus, with the basic foundation to confidently grow and succeed in a competitive environment. For students with less family support, the resolve to "be your best self" will come from your own determination and maturity.

For self-starters navigating a relatively unknown competitive landscape, I hope this book has offered a detailed outline of what America's elite institutions are looking for and how you can best shape your personal experience and academic record to gain admission to your dream school.

Your chosen goal is to attend a top college and you have placed yourself among a highly competitive field of candidates. Your dream is attending an Ivy League college, where, on average, 30,000 students compete for 1,600 coveted admissions slots. Guided by the holistic approach, with or without family support, you will need hooks, hard work, careful planning, and a little bit of luck to realize your dream.

It takes a lot more than a good SAT score and an impressive GPA to gain admission into one of America's top colleges. The dirty little secret is that it is within *your* control to get into America's top colleges.

NOTES

CHAPTER ONE

7 **Before analyzing the incoming class:** Brown University, "Undergraduate Admission—Admission Facts," accessed November 5, 2014, www.brown.edu/admission/undergraduate/about/admission-facts; Columbia University, "Class of 2018 Profile," accessed November 5, 2014, undergrad.admissions.columbia.edu/sites/default/files/2018profile.pdf; Dartmouth College, "Admissions Facts & Advice—Admissions Statistics," accessed November 5, 2014, https://admissions.dartmouth.edu/facts-advice/facts/admissions-statistics; Harvard University, "Admissions Statistics," accessed November 8, 2014, https://college.harvard.edu/admissions/admissions-statistics; University of Pennsylvania, "Incoming Class Profile—Statistics for the Class of 2018," accessed November 8, 2014,

www.admissions.upenn.edu/apply/incoming-class-profile; Princeton University, "Admissions Statistics," accessed November 7, 2014, admission.princeton.edu/applyingforadmission/admission-statistics; Yale University, "Office of Institutional Research—Detailed Data," accessed November 8, 2014, oir.yale.edu/detailed-data.

7 **Across the Ivy League:** Brown University, "Undergraduate Admissions—Admission Facts"; Columbia University, "Class of 2018

Profile"; Dartmouth College, "Admissions Facts & Advice—Admissions Statistics"; Harvard University, "Admissions Statistics"; University of Pennsylvania, "Incoming Class Profile—Statistics for the Class of 2018"; Princeton University, "Admissions Statistics"; Yale University, "Office of Institutional Research—Detailed Data."

9 **The typical class is:** Brown University, "Undergraduate Admissions—Admission Facts"; Columbia University, "Class of 2018 Profile"; Dartmouth College, "Admissions Facts & Advice—Admissions Statistics"; Harvard University, "Admissions Statistics"; University of Pennsylvania, "Incoming Class Profile—Statistics for the Class of 2018"; Princeton University, "Admissions Statistics"; Yale University, "Office of Institutional Research—Detailed Data."

9 **For instance, Columbia reports:** Columbia University, "Class of 2018 Profile."

CHAPTER TWO

17 **Recent US Census data reveals:** Nate Cohn, "More Hispanics Declaring Themselves White," *New York Times*, May 21, 2014.

21 **Many of these same colleges once had explicit caps:** Jerome Karabel, *The Chosen: The Hidden History of Admission and Exclusion at Harvard, Yale and Princeton* (New York: Houghton Mifflin, 2005).

21 **So it's perhaps no coincidence that:** Quynh-Nhu Le, "Do Admissions Officers Discriminate Against Asian Americans?" *Harvard Crimson*, April 30, 2014.

21 **At Berkeley, where admissions are based:** University of California at Berkeley, "Berkeley Undergraduate Profile," accessed November 8, 2014, opa.berkeley.edu/sites/default/files/UndergraduateProfile.pdf.

21 **Asian Americans make up less than 6 percent:** Ibid. and TheIvy Coach.com, "Ivy League Statistics," accessed November 10, 2014, www.theivycoach.com/ivy-league-admissions-statistics.

22 **According to the Census Bureau:** US Census Bureau, "American Community Survey B-03001," 2013, accessed September 27, 2014.

22 **Recent figures from Yale University:** Yale University, "Office of Institutional Research—Detailed Data."

22 **Meanwhile, the African American student population:** Ibid.

CHAPTER THREE

24 **"The 10 Smallest States by School-Age Resident Population (2012)":** "Digest of Education Statistics, 2012," accessed November 5, 2014, www.nces.ed.gov/pubs2014/2014015_1.pdf.

24 **"The 10 Largest States by School-Age Resident Population (2012)":** National Center for Education Statistics, "Digest of Education Statistics, 2012."

25 **Looking at the latest data:** Princeton University, "Admissions Statistics."

26 **At the other end of the scale:** Ibid.

CHAPTER FOUR

31 **Since many applicants to top colleges:** Brown University, "Undergraduate Admissions—Admission Facts"; Columbia University, "Class of 2018 Profile"; Dartmouth College, "Admissions Facts & Advice—Admissions Statistics"; Harvard University, "Admissions Statistics"; University of Pennsylvania, "Incoming Class Profile—Statistics for the Class of 2018"; Princeton University, "Admissions Statistics"; Yale University, "Office of Institutional Research—Detailed Data."

32 **Dartmouth reported:** Dartmouth College, "Admissions Facts & Advice—Admissions Statistics."

CHAPTER FIVE

37 **According to journalist Dan Golden:** Dan Golden, *The Price of Admission: How America's Ruling Class Buys Its Way into Elite Colleges—and Who Gets Left Outside the Gates* (New York: Three Rivers Press, 2006), 158.

39 **We have demographic data:** University of Pennsylvania, "Incoming Class Profile—Statistics for the Class of 2018"; Princeton University, "Admissions Statistics."

39 **Australia accounts for less than 1 percent:** Institute of International Education, "International Students in the United States," accessed November 6, 2014, www.iie.org/Research-and-Publications/Publications-and-Reports/IIE-Bookstore/International-Students-in-the-United-States.

CHAPTER SIX

41 **Michele Hernandez explains:** Michele Hernandez, EdD. *A Is for Admission: The Insider's Guide to Getting into the Ivy League and Other Top Colleges* (New York: Grand Central Publishing, 1997), 195.

41 **In 2011, the percentage of high school graduates:** National Center for Education Statistics, accessed November 7, 2014, www.nces.ed.gov.

45 **While the majority of college-bound students:** "Freshman Survey: Get to Know Harvard's Class of 2018," *Harvard Crimson*, September 2, 2014.

CHAPTER SEVEN

50 **Based on data from all the Ivies:** Brown University, "Undergraduate Admissions—Admission Facts"; Columbia University, "Class of 2018 Profile"; Dartmouth College, "Admissions Facts & Advice—Admissions Statistics"; Harvard University, "Admissions Statistics"; University of Pennsylvania, "Incoming Class Profile—Statistics for the Class of 2018"; Princeton University, "Admissions Statistics"; Yale University, "Office of Institutional Research—Detailed Data."

48–49 **Hard data on how much race determines:** Rosa Ramirez, "Ivy League Schools Don't Reflect US Minority Ratios," *National Journal*, October 19, 2012.

49 **For example, the Asian American enrolled population:** Harvard University, "Admission Statistics."

CHAPTER NINE

63 **Reviewing data for field of study:** Brown University, "Undergraduate Admissions—Admission Facts"; Columbia University, "Class of 2018 Profile"; Dartmouth College, "Admissions Facts & Advice—Admissions Statistics"; Harvard University, "Admissions Statistics"; University of Pennsylvania, "Incoming Class Profile—Statistics for the Class of 2018"; Princeton University, "Admissions Statistics"; Yale University, "Office of Institutional Research—Detailed Data."

64 **accounting majors was 4,934 males versus 15,245 females:** National Center for Education Statistics.

65 **Describing Wesleyan's admissions process:** Jacques Steinberg, *The Gatekeepers: Inside the Admissions Process of a Premier College* (New York: Penguin Books, 2002), 71.

CHAPTER TEN

79–70 **On average, top colleges field twenty-five sports teams:** Statistic Brain, "NCAA College Athletics Statistics," accessed November 8, 2014, www.statisticbrain.com/ncaa-college-athletics-statistics.

72 **Ivy League colleges have the finances:** "Freshman Survey: Get to Know Harvard's Class of 2018," *Harvard Crimson*, September 2, 2014.

72 **Journalist Daniel Golden also observes:** Golden, *The Price of Admission*, 153.

CHAPTER THIRTEEN

105 **I created the list through careful analysis:** "National University Rankings"; "National Liberal Arts College Rankings"; "Top 100—Lowest Acceptance Rates," *US News and World Report*, accessed November 8, 2014, colleges.usnews.rankingsandreviews.com/best-colleges/rankings.

112 **The overall data on selective colleges includes:** Ibid.

112 **Cooper Union has:** *US News and World Report*.

112 **Interestingly, only the forty-five *most* competitive:** Ibid.

112 **For well-respected colleges:** Ibid.

112 **The following information is for the Class of 2016**: Ibid.

121 **For the Class of 2017 applying to the Ivy League:** Brown University, "Undergraduate Admissions—Admission Facts"; Columbia University, "Class of 2018 Profile"; Dartmouth College, "Admissions Facts & Advice—Admissions Statistics"; Harvard University, "Admissions Statistics"; University of Pennsylvania, "Incoming Class Profile—Statistics for the Class of 2018"; Princeton University, "Admissions Statistics"; Yale University, "Office of Institutional Research—Detailed Data."

121 **For Harvard's Class of 2018:** Theodore Delwhiche, "Harvard Makes Admissions Offers to 5.9 Percent of Applicants to the Class of 2018," *Harvard Crimson*, March 27, 2014, www.thecrimson.com/article/2014/3/27/regular-admissions-class-2018/.

122 **For instance, looking at yield for 2017:** Brown University, "Undergraduate Admissions—Admission Facts"; Columbia University, "Class of 2018 Profile"; Dartmouth College, "Admissions Facts & Advice—Admissions Statistics"; Harvard University, "Admissions Statistics"; University of Pennsylvania, "Incoming Class Profile—Statistics for

the Class of 2018"; Princeton University, "Admissions Statistics"; Yale University, "Office of Institutional Research—Detailed Data."

127 **"Ivy League Early vs. Regular Admissions Statistics":** "Ivy League Statistics," TheIvyCoach.com, accessed November 8, 2014, www.theivycoach.com/ivy-league-admissions-statistics.

CHARTS

10 **Average Gender Makeup at Top Colleges for the Class of 2016:** Harvard University, "Admissions Statistics."

13 **Racial Makeup of the Dartmouth Class of 2017:** Dartmouth College, "Admissions Facts & Advice—Admissions Statistics."

23 **Geographical Makeup of the Dartmouth Class of 2017:** Ibid.

33 **Percentage of Legacy vs. Non-Legacy Students for Dartmouth Class of 2017:** Dartmouth College, "Admissions Statistics."

42 **Family Income Level—Harvard Class vs. US Population:** "Freshman Survey: Get to Know Harvard's Class of 2017," *Harvard Crimson*, September 4, 2013; US Census Bureau, "Current Population Survey," *2012 Annual Social and Economic Supplement*; and Nick Kasprak, "Percentage of Taxpayers with AGI over $500,000," Tax Foundation, January 7, 2013, accessed November 11, 2014, www.taxfoundation.org/blog/monday-map-percentage-taxpayers-agi-over-500000.

BIBLIOGRAPHY

Aloi, Daniel. "Class of 2017 Reflects Increases in Diversity." *Cornell Chronicle,* August 15, 2013.

Bostock, Mike, and Neil Irwin. "Which Colleges Do Students Pick?" *New York Times,* September 3, 2014.

Crotty, James Marshall. "Yale Application Reader Reveals 4 Proven Tips for Ivy League Admission." *Forbes,* September 30, 2014.

Henderson, C. W. *Open the Gates to the Ivy League: A Plan B for Getting into the Top Colleges.* New York: Penguin Group, 2013.

Irwin, Neil. "Why Colleges with a Distinct Focus Have a Hidden Advantage." *New York Times,* September 4, 2014.

Jager-Hyman, Joie. *B+ Grades, A+ College Application: How to Present Your Strongest Self, Write a Standout Admissions Essay and Get into the Perfect School for YOU—Even with Less-Than-Perfect Grades.* Berkeley: Ten Speed Press, 2013.

Newport, Cal. *How to Be a High School Superstar: A Revolutionary Plan to Get into College by Standing Out (Without Burning Out).* New York: Broadway Books, 2010.

Rothman, J. D. *Neurotic Parent's Guide to College Admissions.* Pasadena: Prospect Park Media, 2012.

Stabiner, Karen. *All Girls: Single-Sex Education and Why It Matters.* New York: Riverhead Books, 2002.

Wissner-Gross, Elizabeth. *What Colleges Don't Tell You (and Other Parents Don't Want You to Know).* New York: Plume, 2007.

ACKNOWLEDGMENTS

A generation ago, with little exposure to America, I applied to selective American colleges with minimal stress and relative ease. It was a gentler, less competitive landscape. Twenty-five years later, I revisited that landscape as my daughters applied to college. While uncertainty is never relaxing, their application process was interesting, a learning experience, and ultimately successful. I believe that college admissions should and can be a positive rather than stress-laden experience and hope this book will reflect that and help make your college application process easier.

I would like to thank my friend and publisher, Judith Regan, for asking me to write this book. There is much laughter in our friendship, and writing this book was an enjoyable experience. Also at Regan Arts, I would like to thank my editors Michael Moynihan, Lynne Ciccaglione, and Gretchen Spiegel for their support and hard work.

Family and friends have always been central in my life and I am most grateful for them. Particular thanks to my mother and to the dear friend who read the manuscript and provided valued comments. For over twenty years, my daughters have been my source of inspiration, learning, and pure joy. Finally, this book would simply not have happened without my husband, Jay Itzkowitz—we met in Harvard Yard more than thirty years ago and went on to explore the world together. It has been an amazing journey and I thank you.

INDEX

INDEX

INDEX

INDEX

TOP 50 Colleges

THE BEST	Amherst Bowdoin Middlebury Pomona Swarthmore Williams
THE NEXT BEST & THE SOLID MIDDLE	Bates Bryn Mawr Carleton Claremont Colby Colgate Davidson Grinnell Hamilton Harvey Mudd Haverford Mount Holyoke Pitzer Scripps Smith Trinity Vassar Washington & Lee Wellesley Wesleyan
THE REST	Bard Barnard Bucknell Centre Colorado College Connecticut College Denison Dickinson Franklin & Marshall Gettysburg Holy Cross Kenyon Lafayette Macalester Oberlin Occidental Sewanee Skidmore Union College University of Richmond Whitman

TOP 50 Universities

THE BEST	Caltech Harvard MIT Princeton Stanford Yale
THE NEXT BEST	Brown Columbia Cornell Dartmouth University of Chicago University of Pennsylvania
THE SOLID MIDDLE	Carnegie Mellon Duke Georgetown Johns Hopkins Northwestern NYU Rice University of California, Los Angeles University of California, Berkeley University of Michigan, Ann Arbor University of Southern California University of Virginia Vanderbilt Washington University
THE REST	Boston College Boston University Brandeis Case Western Reserve College of William & Mary Emory Lehigh Northeastern University Notre Dame Penn State Rensselaer Polytechnic Institute Tufts Tulane University of California, Davis University of California, Irvine University of California, San Diego University of California, Santa Barbara University of Illinois, Urbana-Champaign University of Miami University of North Carolina, Chapel Hill University of Rochester University of Wisconsin, Madison Wake Forest Yeshiva University